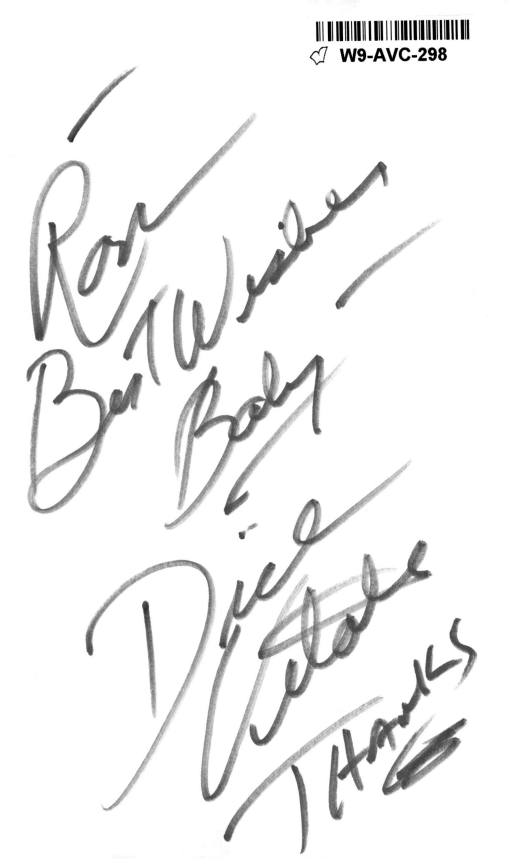

Ron
Best Wishes
Body

Dick Vitale

THANKS

Campus Chaos

Why the Game I Love Is Breaking My Heart

by Dick Vitale
with Dick Weiss

TimeOut Publishing
Indianapolis

Contents

Dedication

I want to dedicate this book to six beautiful people who have played vital roles in my professional TV career: Chet Simmons (the first President of ESPN) and Scotty Connal (Vice President of Production) who took a chance on me and gave me my break in TV; Jim Simpson for his assistance in teaching me the finer points of being a TV analyst; Bob Ley for offering insights into how to handle studio work; Mike Soltys for teaching me how to navigate the world of media relations; and Howie Schwab, a genuine Rolls Roycer who has helped me so much behind the scenes with his brilliant research and analysis. —**DV**

To my parents, Dick and Barbara Weiss, who put up with all my trips to the Palestra so I could develop a love of college basketball and then helped me achieve my dream of becoming a sportswriter by sending me to journalism school at Temple University. And to my wife, Joan, who has been my best friend for more than 30 years and was the driving, inspirational force behind this project. —**DW**

Acknowledgments

I would like to thank all the people behind the scenes —the sports information directors, statisticians, public relations people and the secretaries in college basketball offices across America —who have made my life easier by providing me with a wealth of information that I've been able to share with the fans of college basketball.

I also want to thank all the beautiful people at ESPN and ABC, from the administrators, producers and directors to the play-by-play talent, technicians and everyone involved, for helping me enjoy the greatest job in the world—working on TV talking about the game I love.

I want to thank our publisher, Steve Carroll, of TimeOut Publishing in Indianapolis. Thanks also to Roy Judelson and Sue Lipton, Alex Alton of IMG, and to our editor, Norb Garrett of *Sport* magazine, for his talented efforts in editing this book.

A very special thanks to my wife Lorraine and my daughters Sherri and Terri; and to Dick Weiss for being so easy to work with and proving that in the sports world you can be a success while at the same time being a great person. —**DV**

Thanks to my wife, Joan Williamson, who spent tireless hours helping to shape, research and edit this manuscript; Dick Vitale and his family for their friendship and support; to Norb Garrett of *Sport* magazine and his associates, John Roach, Darryl Howerton, Steve Gordon, Rob Julavits and Mike Elkin; and to Steve Carroll, who has pulled it all together.

Thanks to Mike Sheridan of Villanova for his common sense; and to all the many friends gained along the way...Larry Donald and Dan Wetzel of *Basketball Times*; Terri Thompson, Adam Berkowitz, Barry Werner and Leon Carter of the *New York Daily News*; Bob Ryan, Steve Richardson, Robyn Norwood, Andy Bagnato, Malcolm Moran, Mark Blaudschun, Steve Wieberg, Howard Garfinkel, Kevin McKenna, Frank Morgan, Rick Troncelitti, John Salvo, Sam Albano, Mike Flynn, Tom Pecora, Steve Kirchner, Mike Saab, Brian Morrison, Al Featherston, Caulton Tudor, Tom Abatemarco, Gene Whelan, Dave Gavitt, Mike Tranghese, Tim Tolokan, Mike Enright,

Charlie Pierce, Bill Brill, Bobby Gonzalez, Tom Healy, Rob Wilson, John Feinstein, Ken Denlinger, Mike Wilbon, Marty Tirrell, Ken Thompson, Peter Brown, Lesley Visser, Diane Weiss, Sig and Lynn Morawski, Joe, Betty Ann, Tyler and Devon Cassidy, Jerry McLaughlin and The Guys. —DW

I owe a great deal of gratitude to all the coaches in my life, especially Dick Vitale, Ron Felling, Lou Henson, Bob Hull, Brian Dutcher, Steve Yoder, Johnny Orr, Del Harris, Rob Judson, Glen Korobov, Don Eddy, Dave Casstevens, Sam Wright, Bill Granse, Sam Dixon, Jeff Strohm, Danny Beard, Gene Bartow, Murry Bartow, Kirk Champion, Itchy Jones, Jim Hallihan, Rick Wesley, Homer Drew, Rich Herrin and most especially to my parents, Madge E. Carroll and R. Bruce Carroll, who was recently inducted into the Illinois Basketball Coaches' Association (IBCA) Hall of Fame as a player. I am extremely grateful to my partner, Chris Amore; and to Dick Weiss, Norb Garrett, Doug Carroll, and Harry Benson for their writing and editorial skills. A special thanks is due Alyssa Garrett, and also to my wife and daughter, Terri and Peyton Carroll, for their patience, understanding, encouragement and support.

I also extend my appreciation to Charles Alberta, Doug Altenberger, Dr. James Anderson, Dick Brown, Ed Buerger, Rod Cardinal, Lynn Carroll, Roger Carroll, Ray Compton, Joe Falls, Jeff Fanter, George Fisher, Bill Glode, Dr. Edward Grogg, John Guthrie, Bob Hammel, Mike Hatfield, Mike Hefron, Tim Hofferth, Jim Host, Scott Hutton, Marc Kidd, Dr. Kevin Kruse, Jim Livengood, Matt Loveless, Dr. Tom McGreal, Craig and Lori Martin, David Mills, Bob Palan, Dr. James Parsons, Dale Ratterman, Tom Rutter, John Stote III, Steve Wells, Keith Wendland and Bob Younglove. Also to Patrick J. Amore Sr., Patrick J. Amore Jr., Steve Arnold, Rose and Lou Balogh, Kevin Brady, Beth Broderick, Steve Cosler, Andy Curtin, Mike Fender, Steve Ford, Kris Gebhardt, Gary Huffman, Kevin and Sheila Johnson, George and Julie Kitcoff, Lloyd Millikin III, Don Palmer, Keith Rowe, Tim Rowe, Tim Schlichte, Ron Tsoumas, Ron Voss, Scott Vail and Dr. Jeffrey Yocum. And, finally to all my friends at the Sports Ambassadors and the Fellowship of Christian Atheletes—SC

Foreword

In his 20 seasons on ESPN and ABC, Dick Vitale has been synonymous with college basketball. Through his passion and devotion to the game, Vitale has earned an ever-growing following with an enthusiasm for the game, its players and coaches never before seen in television.

Having coached at the high school, collegiate and professional levels, Vitale brings an insider's perspective to each broadcast, and his lifelong relationships with the administrators, coaches and players provide him a wealth of knowledge few can equal.

Over the years, Vitalisms such as "Diaper Dandy" and "PTPer" have become as much a part of the game as "jump shot." An eternal teenager, Vitale has a spirit that rubs off on anyone within earshot, a fact represented by the legions of fans that show up at games sporting bald domes and waving signs of support.

But behind every "get a TO, baby" and the "slam, jam, bam" resides in Vitale a growing concern for the sport that reels when yet another misguided underclassman announces he's going pro or a new recruiting or academic scandal arises. As much as Vitale is a fan courtside, he's also a champion of the game away from it, spending countless hours lobbying for rules changes or talking with athletic directors about ways to improve the game.

Being so close to the sport, Vitale is infinitely aware of the big-business pressures that affect it today, from the billions of dollars spent by television networks to the controversy surrounding the entrance exam requirements.

And having played and coached basketball, he truly cares about the kids and knows that the success of the sport rides on the shoulders of those student-athletes who proudly wear their school colors into battle.

Here are Vitale's heartfelt thoughts on how to halt the off-court technical fouls of the sport he loves so deeply.

For all of you die-hard college hoop fanatics, Dick Vitale's book, *Campus Chaos*, is a must read!

Rudy Martzke

USA Today

I loved watching Elton Brand play for Duke. I know he was the No. 1 pick in the 1999 NBA draft, but I still wish he would have stayed in college for more than two years. Photo 1-1. facing page (AP Photo).

Chapter

1

See You in September?

The early exodus of kids to the pros is hurting
not only the college game but also the NBA

If Brandon Bender has his way, he won't ever become one of my Diaper Dandies. Bender, a 6-foot-9-inch center from Louisville's Ballard High, is already talking about leaving high school for the National Basketball Association draft if he has a good season. But he wanted to take it one step further than Kobe Bryant and Kevin Garnett. He's thinking about leaving after the 11th grade. That just blows my mind.

The NBA is sticking a dagger into the heart of college basketball, and there's blood everywhere. There are still too many defections to the pros by high school seniors and college underclassmen. The numbers may not be as crazy as they were in 1997, when 39 players declared for early admission, but seven of the first ten players to go in the NBA's 1999 draft were either college underclassmen or, in the case of 6-11 center Jonathan Bender (no relation) of Picayune, Miss., a high school senior.

The tidal wave has even hit Duke. The Blue Devils, who had never had a player declare early for the NBA draft, lost three underclassmen after last season— sophomore center Elton Brand, sophomore guard William Avery and freshman Corey Maggette. Senior Trajan Langdon graduated and was earmarked for the NBA.

The news was a total shocker to me. Duke is the one program I thought never would have star players leaving early for the NBA or have key players transferring. Just shows you how times are changing. Corey Maggette playing 17 minutes a game and leaving Duke University? Get real.

He had never even thought about leaving early until he read a story in the *Chicago Tribune* in which several anonymous NBA general managers, scouts and coaches said they would consider picking him No. 1 if he came out. Wonder if they watched the national championship game when he played only 11 minutes.

But still, any player leaving Duke early is a shock to me, even Elton Brand whose stock will never be higher. Duke is the one school that makes me say "Wow." This is the ideal program. It really represents all that's good in college athletics...student-athletes who are proud to be there, who stay

Mike Krzyzewski won't be able to hug Corey Maggette (50) and Will Avery (5) anymore. Both left this class program early for NBA dollars. At least Chris Carrawell (23) will still be a Dukie. Photo 1-2. (AP Photo).

four years and graduate. In fact, the Blue Devils, who had won two NCAA titles and been to the Final Four five times in the '90's, looked as if they were on the verge of creating another dynasty.

All that talk has been put on hold for now. It was one thing when Brand left. He was the National Player of the Year. But nobody expected Avery to wave bye-bye. And surely no one was ready for Maggette to bolt.

Duke set a record in the 1999 draft by having four players selected in the first 14 picks. Never before had four kids from one school ever been drafted in the first round. Six times there have been three kids drafted, Kentucky being the last in 1996. But four are unreal; it just shows that Duke was loaded with great talent. Here's how it went down:

- Brand went No. 1 to Chicago.

- Langdon went No. 11 to Cleveland.

- Maggette went No. 13 to Seattle, then traded to Orlando.

- Avery went No. 14 to Minnesota.

To me, the notable thing in this draft was that Chicago went for the sure ten-year NBA player, Elton Brand. I think there were three ten-year players in this draft —Brand, Wally Szczerbiak and Andre Miller —quality guys who will never be an area of concern for a coach when he goes to bed at night. These players have good basketball skills as well. They should be very coachable and will give any team a solid ten years, although they may not be superstars.

Some players failed to meet their own expectations in the draft. I'll say it again. Corey Maggette and William Avery made a major mistake by leaving. Had they come back to school, their stock would have risen higher and higher.

You know what really bothered me? I ran into Corey's mother and father at the ACC Tournament and they told me,

Steve Francis of Maryland would have been a first-team member of my All-Rolls Royce squad this year. Instead, he'll be slammin' and jammin' for the NBA Houston Rockets after being traded by Vancouver, which made him the second pick in the draft. Photo 1-3. (AP Photo).

no way is Corey leaving. They had to be broken-hearted, and it was the system that encouraged that to happen.

Maggette kept slipping in the draft, and now he'll have to learn how to play. He needs on-the-job training, but at least he'll get paid while he's learning. I don't blame a kid for doing that. Nonetheless, at Duke he was part of a marquee program, he had great visibility, and he was at a class school. He could have earned a class degree. To throw all that away for instant gratification blows my mind, especially when his stock could have risen had he stayed.

As if all these early entries to the pros weren't devastating enough for Duke, center Chris Burgess, another player from that great sophomore class, decided to transfer to Utah after his father said he had slipped as a pro prospect since arriving at Duke. People have been burned at the stake for saying less — at least in Durham.

Duke is now just another victim of an epidemic that's sweeping this sport. Think about some of the guys who walked out the door early— Lamar Odom of Rhode Island, Steve Francis of Maryland, Richard Hamilton of Connecticut, Ron Artest of St. John's, Shawn Marion of UNLV, Baron Davis of UCLA, all in addition to Brand, Avery and Maggette of Duke. That hurts.

And it wiped out my potential first-team All-Americans...Brand and Maggette, then add Lamar Odom, Richard Hamilton, Baron Davis and Steve Francis. How's that for a Super Six? Instead, my 1999 preseason All-America team was Scoonie Penn of Ohio State, Courtney Alexander of Fresno State, Quentin Richardson of DePaul, Chris Porter of Auburn and Kenyon Martin of Cincinnati. For my second team, I went with Mateen Cleaves of Michigan State, Michael Redd of Ohio State, Terence Morris of Maryland, Mark Madsen of Stanford and Troy Murphy of Notre Dame, not exactly household names, but good, solid players.

Just imagine the excitement if Steve Francis or Elton Brand had returned for another season. Their reputations were so big. But I think they are too quick to take that name recognition to the next level. They're so impatient. Really, it blows my mind.

If Duke had everyone back to go with the new recruiting class it had, it would have made a run at being one of the great teams of all time. We'd have been talking about that team with the UCLA teams of Lew Alcindor, as well as those of Bill Walton, and with the unbeaten Indiana team of 1976. You could have put them in that category. Seven of the first ten in the draft were underclassmen. Again, I am stunned, but that's the trend. That's a problem we've got to hope and pray will change. We've got to see something happen so these kids will stay in school.

I got a big kick out of Tom Weir's column in *USA Today* where George Raveling, Nike's director of grass roots operations, suggested that he wants a developmental league. George feels that if each NBA team expanded its roster to include a 'B' team, they could even use those teams as pre-game events to the actual NBA games.

I agree with him, but Georgie, baby, you must not have read my first two books in which I suggested a developmental league where these entry-level rookies could not only play but also would learn a vocation. I don't know how many times I've talked about having that subsidized by the NBA. If players aren't staying in school, they don't get a chance to be marketed. They don't develop that name. They don't develop that visibility.

That's why I liked Cleveland's draft so much. They took three seniors, Andre Miller of Utah, Trajan Langdon of Duke and A.J. Bramlett of Arizona. They got three solid, quality guys who come to play, know how to play and never give you a problem. In the NBA, where shooting is a problem, Langdon will make shots coming off the bench. He'll definitely be an offensive weapon for Cleveland.

Marty Blake, the NBA's director of scouting, just shakes his head when he thinks about how this insanity will fill the league with teenage millionaires.

"Every time a kid has a good game, there's someone telling him to come out —when usually just the opposite is true," Marty says.

Why this rush to leave college? Have you looked at NBA salaries lately? Kevin Garnett signed a $128 million contract to play with the Minnesota Timberwolves, the richest contract in NBA history, for now. Shaquille O'Neal has a $120 million deal with the Los Angeles Lakers. The Miami Heat is paying Alonzo Mourning $112 million. The Cleveland Cavs are paying Shawn Kemp $107 mil and Juwan Howard is getting $101 mil from the Washington Wizards. They are all in their 20's.

After Brand announced he was leaving, Krzyzewski said it was a no-brainer. Mike took a totally different view when Avery decided to follow in Brand's footsteps. He said publicly that he was not in favor of Avery's leaving. He went on to say that he had done extensive research and felt that the draft wouldn't be in Avery's best interest. Avery's AAU coaches, who made their own phone calls to pro scouts and GMs, felt otherwise and advised Avery's mother that her son had lottery written all over him.

In a lot of ways, Duke is probably lucky this hadn't happened before. Grant Hill definitely could have gone early, but he stayed four years. Christian Laettner could have gone, but he stayed. Now great players staying in school is the exception rather than the rule. And this trend is what's destroying the college game — and breaking my heart.

How will Duke be after the exodus? Its level should drop a little. But don't shed too many tears for Mike Krzyzewski. He simply went out and signed four more McDonald's All-Americans — forward Carlos Boozer Jr. from Juneau, Alaska; guard Jason Williams of St. Joseph's in Metuchen, N.J.; a 6-10 shot-blocker, Casey Sanders, from Tampa, Fla.; and Mike

Dunleavy Jr., the son of the Trail Blazers' coach, from Portland, Ore. That should keep Duke in the thick of the ACC race.

When Coach K, who had his hip replaced in April, got out of bed to speak to the school's basketball celebration at Cameron Indoor Stadium, he said Duke basketball was bigger than any one player, coach or team. But some of the diehard fans acted as if they weren't so sure. There were even some scattered boos when Avery was introduced. Harmony returned only after the introduction of older Duke players Chris Carrawell and Shane Battier.

Battier, the only member of that top-ranked sophomore class to stay around, feels the mass exodus of underclassmen is just a sign of the times. He did the whole AAU circuit and national All-Star game scene. He was Mr. Basketball in Michigan when he played for Detroit Country Day.

"I remember watching Chris Webber and Glenn Robinson play in the McDonald's All-America game," he says. "A couple guys from that game went pro early, but most of them stayed four years. By the time I arrived, more than half the players were talking about leaving college early and some were talking about going right to the pros."

Carrawell, a senior, played with Tim Thomas and Stephon Marbury and thinks Maggette is as physically gifted as either one. He just wonders if another year might have helped him.

"You look at Vince Carter of North Carolina," he says. "He came out after his junior year and was the Rookie of the Year in the NBA. If he had left after his freshman year, he would not have been doing the things he's doing now."

I am in total agreement. And the NBA-champion San Antonio Spurs proved me right. Who were the two stars that led the Spurs over the Knicks? David Robinson and Tim Duncan. And what do they have in common, other than just being extraordinarily gifted 7-footers? They not only went to college, they went all four years. They didn't leave early. And they learned how to win.

Let me say this. Kevin Garnett and Kobe Bryant are brilliant, brilliant players, but as confident as they are, they haven't learned the essence of winning, what shot selection is about, what clock management is about, what's involved in making other players better, how to get the ball to the right guy at the right time. All of that comes with game experience. People can quote you all the statistics about young pro players. But if a guy plays 30 minutes, he'll get some numbers. He'll get numbers because of the 24-second clock and the transition game. I don't want to hear about statistics. I want to see the bottom line.

A kid learns to play to win in the intense, competitive games that are played in college. That's what a lot of players who leave early never have had. There's a special feeling that takes place in marquee games, when you're playing with all that pressure to win.

Players like Robinson and Duncan had it at the Naval Academy and at Wake Forest. And when their four years were over, they walked down the aisle in caps and gowns and received their diplomas, as well as their All-America plaques. They didn't leave early, but they're not starving, man. They're making mega, mega dollars. Robinson is a future Hall of Famer, and Duncan, in my opinion, has become the best player in the NBA. And he's only played two years. He may not be spectacular, but he makes all the right plays at the right times. I've loved him from day one.

I'll never forget what Bernie Lincicome, a columnist out in Chicago, wrote about him. When Wake Forest played in the Great Eight at the United Center in Duncan's junior year, I picked up the paper and Bernie had written, "Oh, yeah, here comes another one of those imaginary guys, built-up, hyped-up superstars —Tim Duncan —who will be the next Danny Ferry."

Well, let me tell you this, a lot of people wish they had the career Danny Ferry had. He stayed at Duke all four years, played ten years in the NBA, and made all those bucks. I'll trade with you, Danny, any day of the week. But, Danny, get a better 'do, man. I don't like that 'do versus mine.

USA Today crunched some numbers regarding NBA drafts and found some trends that absolutely upset me. In eight of the last ten drafts, early entry players picked in the first round have had longer careers than the first-round college seniors who were chosen in the same year. Of the nine players who took the biggest gamble in the last ten years, entering the draft straight out of high school, seven were actually selected. For those who do attend college, the numbers indicated that the players who leave school earlier do better in the draft. In the last ten years, the draft success rate has been 62 percent for college freshmen and sophomores compared to 43 percent for juniors.

The rookie wage scale ranged from $2.679 million for the first player chosen to $535,600 for the 29th and last pick in the first round. All first-round contracts are guaranteed money. The minimum salary for all rookies in 1998 was $287,500. Not bad, when compared to the latest census figures that showed the average annual salary for college graduates was $40,478. Right now, the NBA has a rookie salary cap that lasts five years for players entering the league in 1999. After that, even with the new collective bargaining agreement, it's a relative free-for-all.

And everyone's jumping in. Allen Iverson of the 76ers, Ray Allen of the Bucks, Antoine Walker of the Celtics, Kobe Bryant of the Lakers and Shareef Abdur-Rahim of the Grizzlies all signed for the maximal multiyear deal worth $71 million.

Everybody wants to start the time clock so he can cash in on the second contract. These are mega, mega bucks, especially for youngsters. I can't deny that. Only some Silicon Valley superstars are in the same economic league. But these young ball players see only the immediate money and don't look beyond the short term. This definitely bothers me.

Stats can be misleading and in this case they are. Those salaries go to a very tiny percentage of the draft pool, the ultimate PTPers...prime time performers. Of the approximately 2,000 players in the pool this year, 58 were draft picks. Of that number, only the top 13 became instant millionaires. These players are prodigies. They would have been megastars whenever they came out, and they're not a representative cross-section of all NBA players.

For every Kevin Garnett, there's a Ronnie Fields — a high school Rolls-Roycer who played with Garnett at Chicago's Farragut High. Fields, who originally signed a letter of intent with DePaul but was not admitted, declared himself eligible for the 1997 draft but withdrew before draft day. Most recently, he was playing in the Continental Basketball Association (CBA) and trying to make it to the Bigs the hard way.

How did all this underclassman and high school stuff get started? It's called the Spencer Haywood Rule. Haywood was a star on the U.S. Olympic team in Mexico City in 1968 when he was a sophomore at the University of Detroit. After playing out his junior year, he signed with the American Basketball Association (ABA), which had no rules against signing players whose class had not graduated.

But after playing just one year for Denver, Haywood decided he wanted to switch to Seattle in the rival NBA because he was offered big bucks by Sonics' owner Sam Schulman. But he had yet to go through the NBA draft and some of the other owners objected. So he went to federal court, and a judge declared the draft rules improper because they didn't allow for a player to turn pro whenever he wanted.

As a result, the NBA established the hardship draft for underclassmen. College basketball players have been using this ruling ever since. Frankly, I'm surprised this same principle has not yet been challenged in professional football. In the NFL, a player cannot be drafted until after he has spent three years out of high school.

Look, I can understand why somebody like Kobe Bryant left school early. For somebody who can do it, that's the American way. Why rip him? No matter what job you have in life, if somebody had come to you while you were in college and said, "We'll give you OJT—on-the-job training — at $2 mil a year," what would you do? Bye-bye, college. Some of these guys who leave early will make money. But they're the rare exceptions.

Statistics show that one out of 10,000 players in organized basketball will make it to the pros. The other 9,999 would improve their odds for success by pursuing their education so they have something to fall back on. What is more important to me is how young people define success. If it's just the money a kid is after, then I would tell him to put on the expensive suit, pick up the briefcase and head for Wall Street. But he'd have to go to college to be prepared for that. I have always believed in the American Dream. I do more than believe in it; I live it every day of my life. My parents taught me the value of an education, and I have tried to bring that home to my daughters.

A college education is such a beautiful thing. It offers you a chance to learn, to grow, to have different experiences that will prepare you to be a success in life. I don't know how you can give up the life of being a college kid. And it's not just me talking. That's what Andre Miller said. Wally Szczerbiak said it. So maybe someone's listening to me.

In 14 of the last 20 NBA Championship Finals, the MVP Award has gone to a player who came out early. Last season's winner, Tim Duncan, was the first four-year college player to win the award in the '90's. The only four-year college player to win the NBA's regular-season MVP in the last 13 years is David Robinson. But I say look at the top teams in the 1999 NBA playoffs. San Antonio had five starters — Robinson,

Duncan, Sean Elliott, Avery Johnson and Mario Elie — who stayed in school four years. Many of the Knicks' key players, like Allan Houston, Latrell Sprewell, Larry Johnson, Patrick Ewing and Charlie Ward all did the same.

But the temptation to go early is definitely there, even for high school seniors. The biggest surprise to me is the high school kids who keep coming out. After the 1998 draft, when Al Harrington of St. Patrick's in Elizabeth, N.J., didn't go until the 25th pick overall, and Rashard Lewis and Korleone Young were second-round selections, you'd have thought that later high school players would have learned. Harrington so far has hardly pulled off his sweats for the Pacers and averaged a meager 2.1 points and 1.9 rebounds in 21 games and didn't even make the playoff roster, others got even less PT.

Day after day, sitting on the bench, just to say they're in the NBA. Many of these guys run the danger of three years and out. It could quickly reach the point where the uniform says CBA instead of NBA. There's no guarantee that just because you're young you're automatically going to get better unless your skills are being tested. And they're not being tested in the NBA every day because practices are usually only an hour and a half and they're usually not as intense as college workouts. Especially during the recent shortened season.

In June 1999, there were two more high school kids in the pool, Jonathan Bender and 6-8 Leon Smith of Chicago King. Bender knows hard times. His father died when he was only 13 and his mother as a single parent raised four kids, including a stepson. She worked at Wal-Mart during the day, went to school at night and at the age of 44 graduated college with a degree in community health sciences.

Bender made a name for himself at the McDonald's All-America Game in Iowa when he scored 31 points, breaking the record set by Michael Jordan. He averaged 25 points, 15 rebounds and six blocked shots. He was selected by Toronto with the fifth pick in the draft, then traded to the Pacers for veteran forward Antonio Davis. In accordance with the NBA collective bargaining agreement, he'll make nearly $7 million over the next three years.

Is he ready? Some pro scouts think he's not strong enough to make the transition to power forward. But he's a good shooter and has experienced some success in informal workouts against pro players, which was enough to encourage him to enter the draft. Indiana was willing to take a chance on him. The only thing I question there is how much playing time he'll get, how much time he'll get to develop. He and Al Harrington, I mean, they could start a high school five over there. It's like a developmental league.

Bender has a world of potential. He's 6-11, very quick, runs like a deer, has range as a shooter and has the skills of a much smaller player. Now he's just got to get stronger physically. Leon Smith was the last pick of the first round, going to the Spurs, who eventually traded him to Dallas. They're rolling the dice there, so they may as well roll it on a kid who can possibly help them.

Atlanta surprised me by drafting Georgia Tech sophomore guard Dion Glover at No. 20 even though he had missed the entire season with a knee injury. All the quotes I read from Atlanta were like, "We have told Dion Glover he should go back to school. He's not yet physically ready for the NBA. Dion Glover should go back to school. He hasn't played for a year and he'd be wise going back to school."

I'd like to know the truth. Was Glover told he would be taken by Atlanta with one of its four picks in the first round, which might have encouraged him to enter the draft?

In general, I wonder what the rhetoric coming out of the NBA offices — encouraging kids to go back to school — really means. I really wonder about that because Glover should still be in college. Such rhetoric is a case of "Do as I say and not as I do."

It's a good thing Bender and Smith were first-round picks. Unlike with a college player, if a high school player declares for the draft, he can't change his mind even if he doesn't sign with an agent. A lot of people aren't aware of this rule, and I think it's absurd and should be wiped from the books.

Even though there were only three high school kids involved in the last NBA draft, that's three too many for me. But some NBA honchos and scouts want to see as many kids as possible declare for the draft, and they let the word out through the grapevine, "Hey, I'll tell you what, if Johnny Jones is available, we'll take him in the top five." That gets out on the streets, and that's what fills the heads of some of these kids. "Hey, Al Harrington, you tell Harrington, man, if he comes out of high school, we got him top ten." You tell that to Rashard Lewis, man. And these leeches who come upon these kids and who want them —these guys on the street who try to get near them — fill their heads up with a lot of nonsense. That's not real.

The bottom line is you see kids get hurt. You can't tell me those high school kids are better off sitting on the pine night after night than they would be playing in college, learning competitive five-on-five basketball. I almost choked on my ziti when I saw that Jamaal Magloire of Kentucky was considering entering the draft after his junior year. How in any way, shape or form could he possibly think about leaving when he averaged seven points a game? At least Magloire, who never signed with an agent, had the good sense to change his mind after testing the waters at the Chicago pre-draft camp.

Maybe he saw what happened with Nazr Mohammed last year. Mohammed was the starting center on Kentucky's national championship team, and when he talked to his coach, Tubby Smith, about leaving after his junior year, Tubby advised against it. But Mohammed went anyway, and he was the last pick in the first round. If he had come back to Kentucky, he might have been an All-American. If he had a big-time year, he could have gone in the top ten of the last draft.

I think these young players sometimes sell out for the short term instead of thinking about the long term. They just aren't sure what they want. So why not let the NCAA help them out so we don't have a Corey Maggette teasing a coach until the last day?

Caulton Tudor, a columnist for the *Raleigh News & Observer* writing in *The Basketball Times*, suggested the NCAA move the deadline for declaring from May 16 to early April so as to maintain some kind of control over the game. Then he goes a step further, saying a rule could be passed stating that any player who doesn't commit in writing to the school for the following season by that date would become automatically ineligible for that season, keeping scholarship funds but not playing. I think that's an excellent idea. You want to give a coach some time to be able to recruit a player if someone else wants to walk out the door.

A rule like this might have made it easier on kids like Lamar Odom who sounded like he had no intention of staying in college when he announced he was leaving the University of Rhode Island for the NBA last May. Odom's life has been as much of a soap opera as "*General Hospital.*" He was a great high school prospect out of New York City but lost his way when he attended three different high schools in his senior year.

The one thing I'll say about him is that given all the things he faced coming out of high school, he very easily could have run straight to the NBA but chose college instead. He originally signed with UNLV, but they cut ties with him after *Sports Illustrated* printed a story questioning the validity of his entrance exam scores. Rhode Island then took a chance on the kid but made him sit out his freshman year.

The pro scouts loved his talent. He had some special moments at Rhode Island, including a 25-foot buzzer-beater to give the Rams a victory over Temple in the Atlantic-10 championship game. Odom was considered one of the top three talents in the draft when he signed a contract with Jeff Klein, an attorney for the New York law firm of Weil, Gotshal and Manges.

But two weeks later, he started getting cold feet. Odom blew off a league-wide physical at the Chicago pre-draft camp. Then he missed workouts with Charlotte and Chicago, displaying the kind of inexplicable behavior that could have cost him mega bucks.

Next thing you know, Odom was back on campus trying to return to college. But there wasn't much Rhode Island could do because Odom had automatically forfeited his opportunity to return as soon as he signed that contract with Klein. Once a kid signs with an agent and is taking some money, there's no way to go back. If the NCAA gave him a waiver, it would have had to do it for everybody else. But it didn't.

Odom has the potential to be extremely successful on the next level, and I'm not the only one who feels that way. He held a private workout on campus for four teams — including the Bulls, who had the first pick — three days before the draft. But Chicago sent assistant coach Frank Hamblen rather GM Jerry Krause or coach Tim Floyd.

Krause gave Odom a backhanded compliment, comparing him to eccentric Dennis Rodman and calling him "a character with character" who was fine once the game started. "As long as the young man is basically a good person — and Dennis was basically a good person —you can see there are different ways of evaluating people," Krause said.

The day before the draft, Odom made two road trips — to Miami and then Chicago. Pat Riley worked him out in Miami and supposedly loved him. The Heat tried to trade up to get him, but they weren't willing to part with P.J. Brown for Vancouver's second pick, so that never materialized. Odom also visited with Krause and Floyd in the afternoon. When he finally got back to the hotel in D.C. late that night, he said he felt relatively confident the Bulls would take him. He guessed wrong and slipped to No. 4, where the Clippers finally selected him.

The Clippers? What a natural progression for Lamar Odom. Of all the places for him to go, he's picked by the Clippers who have had a history of one problem after another. But the bottom line is that the kid is talented. Now he has to learn to separate himself from trying to please all his buddies and be concerned about Lamar Odom and really concentrate on making himself the player he can be. Along with Francis, Odom has superstar potential...the key word being potential. And let's not forget that at the time he was drafted, Odom was 19 years old.

Even though the Bulls took the safe route by picking Brand, I think they made a mistake by passing on Steve Francis. Not that I have anything against Elton Brand. He's a solid ten-year player. But if I'm looking for a superstar, somebody who's going to rock that arena, fill that place with excitement galore, Steve Francis is that guy. Instead, Francis was selected by Vancouver, and it took him only a few minutes to declare that he was less than thrilled to be going to Canada. His bickering led the Grizzlies to trade him to Houston in a huge late-summer deal.

But mark my words, he's got superstar skills. He could have used another year to mature, having spent just one year playing at a four-year college. But nonetheless, you'll see him in plenty of NBA highlights. Another member of my would-have-been All-America team, Baron Davis, went No. 3 to Charlotte. Despite his knee injury in college, he has great upside. The Hornets wanted a point guard, and if he stays healthy, he will be a big factor there.

Is there any way to slow down ol' Uncle Mo, this terrible momentum? I asked an expert on the subject, Shane Battier, one of the few Dukies who elected to stay. Battier thinks 21 would be a nice number.

"If you're old enough to drink, you're old enough to make millions," he says.

That's Billy Joel playing "Piano Man" to these ears, baby. I'm probably in the minority, but I really, firmly believe that David Stern doesn't like seeing these young kids coming into the NBA. Stern is the best commissioner in all of sports. He's marketed the NBA just brilliantly, so when Stern speaks, I listen. And I like what I hear. Stern has suggested that the NBA refrain from drafting anyone under the age of 20. But, the NBA Players Association is against a strict age limit.

"We want something that's fair for those who are ready," says Michael Curry of the Milwaukee Bucks.

Fair, in Stern's mind, might be for the NBA and the Players Association to adopt a plan that would add one year to the rookie wage scale for 19-year-olds, and two years for 18-year-olds. Since players are already locked into the team that drafts them for four years, and a possible fifth since that team can exercise the right of first refusal, Stern hopes that such a plan would at least be a step in the right direction. Will the NBA go along with Stern's suggestion? Only time will tell. But at least he's trying to get a dialogue started.

I really believe that down deep, the NBA sees that the league is hurting. In many cases, there are players who see only the instant gratification of the salaries. Obviously, it all comes down to money. Many of these kids dream of the excitement of playing at the NBA level.

But when you talk to many of the guys who are in that league, they say it's the college days they cherish. If you watch a Duke-Connecticut game, for example, you'll see alumni like Grant Hill and Christian Laettner cheering in the stands because they still want to be a part of that special moment. Yet so many young players throw all of that away just for the dollars, that just blows my mind.

Another option is for pro basketball to take a page from another sport. Duke's Carrawell thinks the NBA should follow major-league baseball's model. "If you don't want to go to school, let's have a minor-league system," he says. "If nobody drafts you out of high school, you've got to stay in school for three years." Amen to that.

When kids sign a major-league baseball contract out of high school, nobody says anything. They're put in the minors for a couple of years where they learn how to play professional baseball. There are a lot of basketball players who are flashy, spectacular, but there are very few guys who know how to play, who know how to pass to the post, or know how to find a good shot. David Robinson knows how to play... Tim Duncan knows how to play... Stockton and Malone, they know how to play.

I have to believe that the NBA Players Association can come up with the same system as major-league baseball to prevent this mass exodus of high school and college talent. If a player wants to come to the NBA out of high school, fine. But if he's not drafted, he plays in college for three years and can't enter the draft again until after his junior year. But he'll be playing and learning the game the whole time.

That's the best way to go. Who benefits from all of this? The athlete, the college game and the NBA. It's a win-win situation. I've long been pushing for a developmental league myself.

Kids play for traveling teams at an early age. Dollars come their way, and the idea that there's money to be made is already being implanted in their minds. It's unfortunate, but let's be real. One of the biggest problems in college athletics is that there are too many kids who don't want to be there. They have no desire to be in college. If you don't want to go to college, so be it. College is not for everyone. College is for the true student-athlete who is prepared, taken the college core curriculum, understands what college is about and wants to be in the college scene.

It's not supposed to be about a kid who comes in and holds a press conference announcing, "Well, I think I'll stay in school about a year, then I'll be ready to go to the NBA." What is college basketball becoming? That's not the purpose of going to college.

But there are too many kids taking advantage of the system. All they want to do is stroke the jumper, run with the football, swing the baseball bat and go to the next level. Their whole dream and goal is the next level, next level, next level. We've got a major crisis in college athletics today, especially in high-profile revenue sports like football and basketball. We're hiding our heads in the sand if we don't think so.

Athletes who really don't want to be in school become a nightmare for the coaching staff. It's a sad commentary when coaches tell me they have guys on their staff whose sole responsibility is to get up in the morning and make sure Johnny goes to class. I thought that when you go to college, that going to class is one of your priorities and it most certainly is one of your responsibilities. It's an absolute joke.

But it happens. My buddy, the late Jim Valvano, told me that when he was at N.C. State, he had one of his staff assigned to taking care of his star center, Chris Washburn. His job was to make sure Washburn got to class on time and took care of his academic responsibilities. One day the phone rang in his office, and on the line was a professor claiming he hadn't seen Washburn at all in class.

Jimmy told me he went bananas and got into a verbal battle with the prof, asking him, "What are you talking about? Washburn has to be there. I know he's there. My assistant's been taking him for breakfast and making sure he attends class."

He found out later that as soon as his assistant dropped the kid off and went back to the office, Washburn would sneak out. Isn't it amazing that in some cases, coaches have to become like babysitters because some of these athletes have no desire to go to class? All they want to do is run with the football or shoot the jumper. That's a sad commentary.

I have said from day one that for players like that I'd like to see the NBA subsidize a developmental league to eliminate the trauma and eliminate the travesty in college academics. Let a kid just go play hoops, learn a trade. I would love it. And I'm not alone.

Paul McMann, a former college professor at Babson, wants to put that concept into effect. McMann is the founder of the Collegiate Professional Basketball League (CPBL), which is set to begin in the fall of 2000 for players ages 17 through 22. The CPBL will offer players a $5,000 signing bonus, a $9,000 annual stipend and a college scholarship that's good for up to eight years.

And he's using Krzyzewski's stance on freshman ineligibility to back his position. Basically, Coach K is against the idea of the league, claiming that while it might be a good move educationally, it wouldn't be long before another league is formed. He feels that a kid might then use leagues like the CPBL to get a head start on any freshmen that would be sitting out, thereby decreasing the pool of players coming to college.

McMann says he wants to meet with NCAA president Cedric Dempsey to find some common ground. He does not want to restrict his idea to non-projectors and academic-risk cases. He has thrown out the idea of offering a $10,000 bonus to players who graduate within four years. No one has taken him all that seriously so far, but that hasn't stopped him from pushing on.

He does not want to be dependent on gate receipts, so he has gone after corporate sponsors and will name teams after them instead of the cities they play in. It seems a bit idealistic, given the fact that the league would be in direct competition with major college hoops while offering only limited financial incentives to players. But stranger things have happened. Look at the *X Games*.

If it's the big money that tempts kids to enter the NBA early, maybe facing the prospect of getting less of it will keep them in college. Mark Kiszla, a columnist for the *Denver Post*, came up with this idea: If the NBA really wants to discourage kids from coming out, why not prorate the salary structure. For example, a player who comes out after high school is entitled to only $250,000 per year maximum. After one year in college, a rookie gets $400,000, and if an athlete comes out in two years, his salary goes to $500,000, etc.

I'd like to propose another solution to the problem of kids leaving college early: Form a blue-ribbon panel composed of coaches and former NBA players —people like Dr. J, Jerry West, John Thompson, David Gavitt. This group would designate the players most likely to be first-round draft choices, and those athletes would be able to borrow $50,000 a year from the NCAA or from a fund put together by the NBA.

If a player borrows that money, he must pay it back after he becomes a professional athlete. Why not allow selected players to borrow up to $50,000 a year if that helps them stay in school? If David Stern and the NCAA got together on this, it could happen. It's obvious that something has to be done.

Krzyzewski says the NCAA has to take more responsibility for the financial situations of its athletes. "I'd hoped the NCAA would look at the needs of players who are here and undergoing temptations," he says. "You would hope a kid is not making this decision [leaving early] because he can't make a car payment or he has some type of a financial problem. We have to come up with a financial solution." Krzyzewski has also said there has to be some dialogue between the NCAA, the NBA and the Players Association

The top ten programs may be able to recruit top-five players, but they can't keep them in school. It's a Catch-22, the better they are, the sooner they leave. Think about what happened at North Carolina. Rasheed Wallace and Jerry Stackhouse helped lead the Tar Heels to the Final Four as sophomores. Then they both left, leaving Dean Smith to rebuild. The Tar Heels got a break because Antawn Jamison was so good as a freshman. They won 21 games but were eliminated in the second round by Texas Tech.

Then, one year later, Jamison and Vince Carter helped Carolina get back to the Final Four as sophomores. When they both moved on, Bill Guthridge was left to rebuild, and people got all over his case when the Tar Heels lost to Weber State in the first round of the Tournament last year.

After Kentucky won the national championship in 1996, Antoine Walker left for the pros after his sophomore season. The next year, after the Wildcats reached the national finals, Ron Mercer also left for the pros after his sophomore season.

But it's not just the NBA that's siphoning kids from the college game. And it's not just Duke that's been affected. If players aren't leaving for the pros, they're leaving for what they think are greener pastures — more PT, better opportunities at another program. No less than eight blue-chippers from marquee programs — including Burgess, Ryan Humphrey of Oklahoma, Adam Harrington of N.C. State, Michael Bradley of Kentucky, Byron Mouton of Tulane and Luke Recker of Indiana —transferred to another college this past year.

And the day a player announces he's leaving, there are two-dozen coaches in America chasing him, which to me is sad. The kids know there are coaches out there just waiting for a kid to say he's a little unhappy and then pounce on him. Maybe if the coaches were a little more patient, kids wouldn't be jumping here, there, elsewhere.

Harrington left N.C. State for Auburn after leading the team in scoring. Humphrey left Oklahoma for Notre Dame after starting almost every game for two years. Mouton transferred to Maryland from Tulane, where he was the team's leading scorer. Burgess figured to be a starter at Duke.

The Luke Recker case had the biggest repercussions. Recker is a 6-6 forward who was Mr. Basketball in Indiana and averaged 16 points a game as a sophomore at IU. He was

Indiana's Luke Recker has left for Arizona where he thinks he stands a better chance of getting to the NBA—why must it always be NBA, NBA, NBA? Photo 1-4. (courtesy *Indianapolis Star*)

a huge fan favorite in Bloomington. But he walked away from a life-long dream and transferred to Arizona because he said his development would be better served in another program.

After the transfer, Recker suffered a tough blow in the summer of 1999 when he was injured as a passenger in an auto accident, but thankfully was OK.

I have a problem when a player uses the excuse of not developing for the NBA as a reason for changing scenery. If Luke was unhappy because of a lack of playing time or not having fun, fine. But don't talk about the NBA as the reason to transfer.

Recker's departure only compounded the team's woes that began when Neil Reed left for Southern Mississippi three years ago, and Jason Collier, a McDonald's All-America center, left for Georgia Tech at semester break in 1997. Hey, Bob Knight has lost players before, and I'm sure he'll lose others. Some 37 players have left by transfer, expulsion or early draft entry in Knight's 28 years as a coach. That has not stopped Knight from winning three national championships and 11 Big Ten titles.

Obviously with the General there are those who love everything he does, and those who dislike his methods. His dissenters were all over him because Indiana failed to advance beyond the second round of the NCAA Tournament for five years up through 1999. In fact, in March 1999, the Hoosiers lost to St. John's by 25 in a second-round game in Orlando, a thorough humiliation.

Knight has spoiled the faithful by winning those national titles and now for some fans making the NCAAs isn't enough. They want it all, every year, and that's just unreasonable. However, Recker's decision to leave set off rumors that Knight might be close to hanging it up if he can't control the state in recruiting anymore. Forget about it. There is no way he steps aside because he firmly believes in his philosophy and still loves the game, even though the recruiting wars are wearing on him.

Neil Reed here with Coach Knight, is among the IU players to have transferred to another program. Coach recently addressed the student body and made these important observations: "Out of 117 scholarships in 28 years, 37 have left and 80 have played four years...32% transferred compared to 38% nationally. The graduation rate for the school is 68%... in basketball it's 79%... of the 80 who have played four years, only three have not gotten a degree." Photo 1-5. (AP Photo).

When Michael Bradley, a promising 6-10 sophomore center, left Kentucky, athletic director C.M. Newton, went public and vented about transfers, claiming there was no loyalty left in college basketball. I've said before that C.M. is the David Stern of college basketball. He's the best. But C.M., I disagree with your feeling that transfers should sit out two years as a deterrent. C.M. spoke about a decline in loyalty after Michael Bradley, Myron Anthony and Ryan Hogan decided to leave. But Kentucky has benefitted from its share of transfers in the past, such as Derek Anderson from Ohio State, Mark Pope from Washington and Heshimu Evans from Manhattan.

I don't think he meant it the way it came out. I think what he was trying to say was that an epidemic is taking place and there must be some way to stop it. His suggestion was to force a kid to sit out two years if he leaves. That's not fair. Coaches have no problem saying adios if they get a better offer from another school, and nobody says they have to sit out a year.

When Anthony, Bradley and Hogan signed with Kentucky, they signed to play for Rick Pitino. Well, Pitino bolted for a mega-buck deal with the Boston Celtics before they ever arrived in Lexington. In my mind, those kids should have a chance before they enroll to go elsewhere. As it is now, if a player enrolls, he's got to follow the rules and sit out a year. You know, in some of the non-revenue sports like golf, tennis and swimming, if you receive a release from a school, you can transfer and be eligible to play immediately.

I'd love to see the rules changed. If a student-athlete is unhappy and the coaches agree with him that it would be best to transfer, then that youngster should not have to sit out a year when he transfers. But, in the case of an athlete who's getting ample PT and the coach doesn't agree with his desire to transfer, then that player should have to sit out one year before being eligible to play at the new school.

Some schools, like Morehead State, are fighting back the only way they know how. Coach Kyle Macy and the athletic director originally refused to give star player Erik Brown, who averaged 19.3 points and made first-team All-Ohio Valley, a release when they got wind of rumors that other schools were tampering with him. Morehead said Brown could transfer, but without a release he could not receive an athletic scholarship from another school in 1999-2000. Afterward, Macy said he wanted to show that mid-major schools like Morehead were not training camps for high majors, however the school eventually relented.

Sometimes kids don't have to wait until high school to be pursued big-time by coaches. Players are being put on pedestals at an early age by scouting services that rate kids before they reach high school. Clark Francis of *Hoop Scoop* lists the top seventh- and eighth-graders in the country each year...talk about Diaper Dandies. But some kids stand out, even at an early age.

Hoop Scoop and *Full Court Magazine* rate middle school players on a regular basis. And because colleges are not allowed to contact players until they enter high school, there have been several reports about schools trying to gain an early advantage. Francis claims that several Division I powers including Kentucky and UCLA all contacted 7-0 junior Tyson Chandler, a top-five prospect from Compton, Calif., Dominguez, when he was in middle school.

Look at Felipe Lopez, who was the National Player of the Year over Allen Iverson when he signed at St. John's out of Rice High in New York City. I still remember when he appeared on the cover of *Sports Illustrated* before he ever played a college game. The school thought it would be a good idea. But Lopez found out quickly that it was hard to live up to the hype. Lopez's decision to stay close to home at St. John's simply added to the pressure.

Sometimes a player is better off going to a program where he can blend in, where he can play with a lot of great players, rather than being forced into being the man as a freshman. Think about the advantages Rasheed Wallace and Jerry Stackhouse had, going to North Carolina, where they could blend in for a year with Eric Montross, Derrick Phelps and company.

Kids have to be affected by what they hear. And by what they're told. Last spring, the *Chicago Tribune* ran a huge story on Lorenzo Thompson, a gifted 6-7 eighth-grader who attended Bethel Christian, a private school, the last two years and who has been the subject of recruiting battles in two of his last three academic years. Thompson had his seventh-grade tuition paid for by a donation from a corporate sponsor.

When the coach, Terry Sawyer, who also helps out with the traveling team Illinois Fire, left Bethel for another job, the financial support ended. Thompson almost left, but Verna Baker, the principal, came up with other scholarship money to pay his eighth-grade tuition.

Thompson won't be finishing his career at Bethel. When the Chicago Public League coaches started to hear about the kid, they jumped all over him. He played for Crane and Farragut — Kevin Garnett's school — in spring and summer events. And the list of interested schools included King, Lincoln Park, Manley, Prosser, Providence-St. Mel, St. Joseph's of Westchester and Westinghouse. The recruiting calls were coming like crazy.

Eventually, Thompson settled on Prosser, an academic school that attracts kids from all over the city. Last year, there were 3,400 applications for 320 slots. Thompson got in based on a number of factors, including teacher recommendations, attendance and athletic ability.

The sophomore coach at Prosser just happens to be Doug Key, who coached Thompson on the Illinois Heat. Their point guard, Carl Marshall, is one of Thompson's best friends. Whether Thompson lives up to all the hype remains to be seen. But he already has a national reputation.

Most kids coming into college are fairly well known before they enter school. Tom Konchalski of *HSBI*, Bob Gibbons, and Clark Francis who run the best scouting services in the country, have turned them into stars by the start of their senior year in high school. I'm as guilty as anybody else in talking about young players, although I sing their praises only after I've seen or read about them. But when you start rating sixth-, seventh- and eighth-graders, you're way over the edge.

The recruiting services are all trying to discover these kids at an early age. Their reasoning? A lot of coaches claim they've missed out on a lot of kids. Then there are the kids who don't work out. I don't hold the scouting services responsible for some of the athletes who don't live up to their early reputations. That's part of the process of growing as an athlete. And part of being great is being able to sustain greatness after expectations are laid on you.

But if you look at the margins of success of the scouting services, you'd be shocked to see the number of times they're right. And to think I coined the term "Diaper Dandies." I just hope the powers-that-be will do something to assure that those Diaper Dandies will be doing their teething in college and not in the pros.

Lamar Odom stayed at Rhode Island just long enough to make a name for himself before leaving for the NBA after just one season. Hope he likes the Clippers. Photo 2-1. facing page (AP Photo).

The Impossible Dream

*As the dollars increase and everybody wants
a piece of the pie, agents and boosters are
undermining the college game*

January 1999: I'm standing in the tunnel just after
doing the Maryland-Duke game at Cole Field House in College

Park, Md., when I notice super-agent David Falk in the Duke locker room. Something about that really felt wrong to me. Falk is one of the most powerful agents in America, the man who helped Michael Jordan make his millions.

That night I just felt that his presence in a locker room really set a bad precedent. And, after learning that Duke's Elton Brand eventually signed with him, that bothered me tremendously. Brand left Duke in April and signed with Falk in May. I have no problem with David. In fact, I truly feel he's one of the best in the business. But I do have a problem with any agent walking into a college locker room.

First, let me throw out a few numbers. The marquee talents in the NBA make big bucks. Falk has numerous clients, including stars such as Patrick Ewing, Dikembe Mutombo, Alonzo Mourning and Juwan Howard, who have contracts that average around $15 million a year. Even if Falk charges only two percent, he could gross close to $30 million a year. With that kind of money, there are a number of people who want a piece of the action. And that's just for basketball. There are 850 agents certified by the NFL Players Association, another 150 agents recognized by the NBA Players Association. Most are trustworthy, but some are not.

"The No. 1 problem in college athletics is agents," Ohio State football coach John Cooper claims.

For a lot of kids, their introduction to agents comes long before they put on that college uniform. There have always been sleazy characters, cruising the playgrounds, hustling kids who are 14 or 15 and have a world of potential. They're approaching kids with cash in their pockets, looking to make a quick hit with somebody they think will be big-time someday.

They'll offer up 100 bucks to some kid who doesn't have a dime in his pocket, who comes from a single-parent family, who has trouble getting three square meals a day. That temptation is hard to turn down. If the kid takes the money, he in turn feels obligated to that agent when and if he hits it big.

Super agent David Falk, is seen here having a laugh with client Patrick Ewing at a Hoya's game. Photo 2-2.   (AP Photo).

These hustlers then think they own the kid down the line. I don't call those guys agents. They have no financial or management training. I call them street clowns. They're hustlers. They're dealers. They're dealing hoops like guys deal drugs.

The temptations are everywhere and can turn into scandals overnight. Look what happened to UMass in 1996. The school had its NCAA Final Four finish wiped from the record books and had to return 40 percent of its Tournament earnings — approximately $150,000 — after All-America center Marcus Camby admitted receiving money and gifts from two street agents. Camby comes from the projects of Hartford, Conn., so you can see how the temptation might have been too strong.

I'm not saying he was right in what he did. But it's pretty tough — unless you live there and have been in that situation — to understand what he went through. But get this: Camby's first would-be agent, John Lounsbury, sued Camby for breach of contract. Lounsbury claimed he gave $40,000 to Camby, members of his family and friends between October 1994 and April 1996. In exchange, he claims, Camby promised to hire him as his agent.

According to Lounsbury's attorney, John Williams, too much emphasis has been placed on the sins of agents and not enough attention has been given to the "greed of these professional athletes." Camby's current agent, Alex Johnson, said Camby never agreed to be represented by Lounsbury. Camby has admitted to accepting $2,000 from Lounsbury and two necklaces and a diamond pendant from Wesley Spears, a Hartford lawyer, who also wanted to represent him. He signed with neither.

Lounsbury didn't limit himself to the Atlantic-10. UConn's basketball program was hit when the NCAA suspended two of its key players — Kirk King and Ricky Moore — in 1997 for accepting airline tickets from none other than John Lounsbury. In December 1997, Lounsbury agreed not to act as a sports agent for five years after cutting a deal with the Connecticut Department of Consumer Protection.

You know, kids blame the agent, but it's a two-way street. These student-athletes have to know right from wrong as well because temptation is everywhere. Just ask Joe Hamilton, quarterback at Georgia Tech. At the Atlantic Coast Conference football media day, Hamilton said there are more agents getting to college players than people think.

"A lot of guys I've known from schools across the nation have gotten away with a lot. They're not in the NFL right now, not playing any more football, but nobody ever knows how they got away with $500,000, a nice car, a nice ride. Nobody ever knows. We try not to do that at Tech at all, but it's hard. It's out there for everybody."

According to Hamilton, an agent's usual modus operandi is to prey on a certain player's hobbies, or befriend him by showing up in the dorm with a pizza. Some players are taking steps to avoid contact. Peter Warrick of FSU and Duke's Scottie Montgomery have changed their phone numbers — more than once. And if you phone Hamilton, one of his roommates will screen the call. But is it enough?

"I just moved and they've already got my number," Warrick told The *Orlando Sentinel.* "They must be the FBI or something."

It seems there have been a lot of agent sightings in Florida as of late. In the spring of 1999, the NFL Players Association accused agent William "Tank" Black of giving money and cars to former Florida players before their college eligibility ran out. That's a crime in the state of Florida, and campus police are investigating along with the NFLPA.

Here's what allegedly went down. Black, who was certified by the NFLPA, has been in the business since 1988. He used to be an assistant football coach at South Carolina before becoming an agent. His first client was receiver Sterling Sharpe. Not a bad start. From there, his client list grew to 40, and his business brings in more than $10 million a year. Not a bad piece of change.

He has recruiters hustling talent all over the Southeastern Conference. Black represented two speedy Florida receivers entering the 1997 NFL draft — Ike Hilliard and Reidel Anthony. When Hilliard's and Anthony's stock skyrocketed leading up to the draft, they talked up Black's company, Professional Management Inc. (PMI), to their former teammates. Four of them — linebackers Jevon Kearse, Johnny Rutledge, Mike Peterson and defensive tackle Reggie McGrew — signed with Black two years later. These were high-profile guys on Bobby Stoops' defense. Kearse was a first-team All-American. Rutledge was also a potential first-round selection.

But things spun out of control after the 1999 draft when Rutledge, who was taken in the second round by the Arizona Cardinals, told *Florida Today* that he had received $500 a month for more than a year from Black during his last season. That was just the tip of the iceberg. The *St. Petersburg Times* followed up those accusations with an expose of its own, accusing Black of allegedly purchasing a $133,500 Mercedes Benz for Kearse on December 31, 1998, two days before the Gators played Syracuse in the Orange Bowl.

If that had gone down, Kearse would have been ruled ineligible for the game. Kearse turned many a head when he drove the Benz to a press conference on January 5, 1999, to announce he was leaving school a year early to go pro. You can imagine how Florida coach Steve Spurrier reacted when he read the *St. Petersburg Times* story. He blew up like a volcano.

I love what Spurrier said, and I love what he did. One thing about Spurrier, man, he speaks his mind. You may not agree with everything he says, but I'll tell you one thing: The guy has integrity. Coaches have to be accountable. Many times, things happen without coaches being aware. They may

Sports agent Tank Black is not one of Steve Spurrier's favorite people after he allegedly signed three Florida football players before their eligibility was up. Photo 2-3. (AP Photo).

have an idea that something's going on, but they are not totally aware. I know one thing about Spurrier and Bobby Bowden of Florida State. They're on their players constantly about staying away from shady characters.

Players weren't born yesterday. They know it's wrong to take $500 a month from a guy. Spurrier was ticked. Those kids might have taken the money, he said, but by doing so they were no longer Gators, and let that be a warning to any other player interested in such mischief.

But Spurrier said, "I'll tell you what we're going to do. You want to play that [money] game? You want to go there? You know that's wrong."

"I don't want them in the school, or to use their alumni contacts later on for anything," he said. "They are not welcome in Gator football. And I'm not blaming just the agent."

Spurrier became my hero that day. His message was clear: They made their beds when they took the cash. The NCAA has praised Florida's efforts, too. Florida athletic officials confirmed that their football players signed forms at least three times during the 1998 season verifying they had not made illegal contact with agents.

In addition to other agent-awareness measures, school officials were stationed outside the Florida locker room in an effort to fend off possible agent-player dealings. Should Florida have been punished? No, according to the NCAA's Bill Saum, who monitors these transgressions. Florida would be clean unless the school had known about the problem in advance and had let the kid play.

In a sign of just how desperate schools are to educate themselves to the trauma of dealing with agents, Florida asked rival Florida State about the school's annual Agent Day, a program in which agents are invited to campus and seniors who have exhausted their eligibility have the chance to meet with them under university supervision.

The program was instituted following FSU's well-publicized agent fiasco in 1994 in what has become known as the "Foot Locker Scandal." The incident occurred when a runner for one of these agents took several players on a shopping spree at a local Foot Locker store. Spurrier was quick to jump on the Seminoles after that, calling them "FSU: Free Shoes U." Now the shoe is on the other foot.

Meanwhile, Black has been defending himself like crazy ever since the story surfaced. His attorney, Leonard Mungo, said Black bought the car but that it wasn't given to Kearse until January 5, three days after the game. He went on to say that Kearse had had no idea about the car until after his eligibility was completed and that there was no agreement to provide the car to Kearse in exchange for his signing with Black. Mungo claimed that the date on the odometer statement was fudged so that the dealership could get credited for a 1998 sale. Kearse stands behind Black, claiming he wasn't offered anything.

Black has since filed a $25 million lawsuit against the NFL Players Association for lost wages and a tarnished reputation, claiming Rutledge, Peterson and McGrew were beaten down and intimidated by campus investigators when they made their statements. He's even petitioned the U.S. Attorney's Office to investigate the union's actions. But he has already lost all four clients and $600,000 in fees.

Black is catching all kinds of flak from various quarters. Atlanta-based agent Ray Anderson accused Black in January 1999 of offering LSU assistant coach Mike Haywood more than $10,000 to secure defensive lineman Anthony McFarland as a client. Black has denied that. In July 1999, Black had his license revoked for three years by the NFLPA. If Black reapplies within that time period, he'll be fined $25,000. This was the most severe penalty imposed by the NFLPA.

Bloody but unbowed, Black has said one of his company lawyers would conduct contract negotiations, in his stead, if the penalty is enforced. However, the dark cloud hanging over

Black has had somewhat of a silver lining. Among the clients who have stayed with him is Vince Carter of the Toronto Raptors, who signed a contract extension.

While Florida might be the latest school to make headlines, the agent problem made headlines two years ago in an altogether unlikely location when trouble surfaced at Penn State, home of Joe Paterno's straight-laced football program. As the Nittany Lions prepared for their usual postseason bowl action, a Houston-based agent named Jeff Nalley tried to get in good with junior running back Curtis Enis by buying him $1,000 worth of clothing at a Harrisburg, Pa. shopping mall. Trouble was, a Harrisburg TV station found out about it and broadcast the story. At first, both Nalley and Enis tried to cover it up, but eventually the truth was exposed.

Enis was suspended for Penn State's final game, a Citrus Bowl appearance against Florida. Nalley was hauled into court, where he pleaded no contest to a charge of unlawful activity by an athletic agent. The judge in Common Pleas Court fined Nalley $10,000 and sentenced him to 100 hours of community service. In October 1998, the NFLPA suspended Nalley for two years. But the damage had already been done. Enis, who had made several All-America teams, left school, entered the NFL draft and was selected fifth overall by the Chicago Bears.

If all this sounds like a soap opera, then it should come as no surprise to you that show business types have gotten involved in college athletics. Rap star Master P put his name onto the sports pages when Heisman Trophy winner Ricky Williams signed with Master P's agency, No Limit Sports. Needless to say, the signing created quite a stir not only in Austin, Tex., but also around the nation. Williams said he was besieged by people telling him not to sign with Master P, that Master P was a businessman, not a sports agent.

But as Williams pointed out, "Master P told me to ask them how much money they made last year."

Master P knows how to make money. A recent issue of *Fortune* magazine lists his net worth at $36.1 million, more than what they report for Michael Jordan. Some speculate that by signing with Master P, Williams slipped in the draft from perhaps the top spot to No. 5. This much we know, New Orleans Saints coach Mike Ditka couldn't have cared if Mother Teresa were representing Williams. He traded the kitchen sink to move up and select Williams.

Turns out those critics might have been right. The contract Williams eventually signed with New Orleans is non-traditional, to say the least. Many agents have labeled it ludicrous. Williams received an $8.84 million signing bonus, the maximum for his draft position. His contract is laced with incentives that could drive it up to $57.3 million in the first four years, but only if he meets all his goals and puts up Terrell Davis-type numbers.

In the first year alone, Williams would have to rush for 1,600 yards — something that has happened only nine times in the '90's — and score 24 touchdowns, half rushing, half receiving, to receive all his bonus money. If Williams holds out for any reason, the club has the right to take back part of his signing bonus. But, hey, it probably made headlines in *Variety*.

Agents are wrong to dangle temptation in front of kids, many of whom know better but unwisely jump on the easy cash. If an agent does things the right way and provides the player with the proper guidance and incentives, fine. I have no problem with the agent taking a percentage. What I despise is any agent who puts money in the hands of a player while the kid is still in school and knowingly puts the kid at risk. Are kids today more prone to temptations? As Bob Knight says, the kids haven't changed, it's just that there are more distractions than ever before.

I want to believe kids are not allowing themselves to be bought, but it's wild what's happening on campus these days. Agents are hiring college kids, girls and middlemen to chat up players, push them in their direction for a finder's fee. Agents tell them, "Get Johnny Jones and we'll take care of you." So they do. Everybody's looking for the quick dollar today. It's just not healthy that these people run around with a few bucks in their pockets trying to entertain kids and steer them to agents. It's bad for the game. Nobody lays anything on you just because you're a super kid. They want to buy your body.

I tell the kids, "Don't be a prostitute. If you can look in the mirror and say, 'I've been doing things the right way,' you can have a great life." If you make it, it'll be super, because you won't have to be obligated to some character that is trying to seduce you and might ruin your reputation. You have only one reputation, and it will be determined by the way you carry yourself." Many guys don't care, and they just tarnish themselves and their families.

It's so hard to control the runners and third-party recruiters who prey on college kids. Schools today are doing just about anything they can to keep distance between the agents and the athletes. Just take a look at the story of Lamar Odom and his former assistant coach (now head coach), Jerry DeGregorio, at Rhode Island. DeGregorio was tight with Odom. He even put him up at his residence for a while Lamar was finishing prep school at St. Thomas Aquinas in Connecticut.

When Odom came to Rhode Island, DeGregorio knew how talented the kid was. He also knew Odom would be besieged by agents and runners, so he tried to help out as some sort of personal bodyguard. Rumor has it when Rhode Island went on the road, the school even registered Odom under a false name at hotels. Even that didn't stop one runner from barging onto the court at the start of practice one afternoon. Odom entered the 1999 NBA draft after just one full season of varsity competition.

St. John's is taking even more precautions. Starting with the 1999-2000 season, the school was considering having its own security guards accompany the Red Storm on road trips. The administration hopes this will keep unsavory characters at bay. This is what we've been forced into?

I like the fact that 23 states have new laws against unlicensed and illegal agent activity. If every state adopted similar legislation it might scare away people who are greedily and fraudulently trying to get their teeth into players. There is no federal legislation to control the problem, so players associations are stepping in to fill the void.

Pro football has taken a strong stance. In March 1999, the NFLPA approved a bylaw that forces an agent to forfeit any fee he receives if it's proven that he offered an illegal inducement to a college player.

The association had already taken some steps when a three-man disciplinary committee, made up of the Dolphins' Trace Armstrong, the Raiders' Richard Harvey and the Vikings' Robert Smith, recommended suspending the license of Cincinnati-based agent James Gould.

Gould was accused of supplying former Michigan safety Marcus Ray with tickets to a jazz festival that included meals and access to a stadium luxury skybox. He was also accused of helping pay for hotel rooms. Gould, who represents 23 NFL players, appealed the ruling and, following the investigation, reached a settlement with the NFLPA that included a $5,000 fine and a retroactive suspension, which ended up being just eight days. According to Gould's attorney, a bank actually provided the tickets and Ray picked them up at Gould's offices.

While acknowledging that Gould assisted in paying for a room, he allegedly did so only after a friend of Ray's mother was unable to use her own credit card for payment. Ray was suspended on September 17, 1998, after Michigan officials learned from the NCAA that he might have made improper contact with Gould and had received extra benefits. The NCAA suspended Ray for six games and ordered him to pay $477.26 in restitution for the tickets to the jazz festival.

Agents can truly mess up a kid's life, but don't get me wrong. I'm not down on all agents. A good agent can be important to a player's success. Not every player is a superstar, you know, and a good agent can make a player look good in workouts. Bill Duffy turned his client, Michael Olowokandi, from a relative unknown at Pacific into the top pick in 1998's draft by featuring his strengths in front of pro scouts.

The flip side occurred in 1999 with Duke's Corey Maggette, who didn't bother to sign with an agent. He flopped in several workouts because he failed to showcase his dramatic strengths, instead shooting air balls from three-point land.

In fact, a lot of the first-round draft picks are now dodging agents altogether. If they get guaranteed money, the contract's ironclad. They're using business managers for shoe deals, marketing deals, commercials and endorsements. The NBA's new salary arrangements and cap limits have brought that change about. You don't have to give a guy five percent because everybody knows what the parameters are. Grant Hill of the Detroit Pistons and Ray Allen of the Milwaukee Bucks hired lawyers — in Allen's case, it was Johnnie Cochran — at $500 per hour to dot the *i*'s and cross the *t*'s on their contracts.

Agents all need to police themselves. One possibility is the formation of an agents association, with members in good standing a must for anyone who wants to negotiate contracts. Agents who violate the rules could be fined or even suspended. Agents should have to register and be certified by the NCAA the same way they are by the NBA and the NFL. Heck, you have to meet criteria to be a lawyer, to be a doctor. This should be no different.

But would this be enough? No. We have to start educating kids before they get to college. If there's a high school kid who is being chased by everybody, who's on everyone's top-ten list, the kid's parents, his high school coach and the guidance counselor have to sit him down and explain his options to him.

Many colleges have beefed up their education programs. Penn State has a panel of on-campus experts designed to do just that. Tennessee football coach Phil Fulmer discusses the same thing in weekly seminars with his seniors. Florida State has two programs. One is an orientation for all incoming freshman athletes. The other is a course called "Professionalism in Sports," which addresses business, agents and financial planning.

Temple has gone one step further, developing an agent-screening program for its football and basketball players with the blessing of the coaches involved. Dr. Michael Jackson, head of the program, talks to all the prospective pro athletes on campus and convinces them that they should have no dealings with agents until after their college careers are over. In the meantime, he collects as much information, brochures, references, etc., as possible from any agent who wants to represent a Temple athlete. Then he passes it along to the athlete, along with names, addresses and phone numbers. Jackson also volunteers to get a short list of agents a player wants to speak with, sets up interviews and even sits in if the athlete so desires. He does this free of charge.

But there may be another solution, one that involves money. A couple years ago, Dave Seigerman, writing in *College Sports* magazine, came out with a more radical solution. Open the door for college athletes to sign with agents while they're still in school. In Seigerman's view, the NCAA needs to take a new look at amateurism. Even the Olympics are paying players these days. Every member of the men's and women's basketball teams received $50,000 to train with the squad in preparation for the 1996 Summer Games in Atlanta.

The NCAA had even looked into the possibility of allowing players to hold jobs during the school year. But then reality set in. And the reality is that with the time schedule an athlete is under, it's impossible to be able to do three things at once; preparing himself as an athlete, going to class and working. The demands are just too great. Right now, schools have off-season training, preseason conditioning and summer league games.

Seigerman proposed that if the NCAA was against the idea of flat-out paying players, fine, but give athletes the opportunity to be paid. Allow them to work. And allow them to sign with an agent. It would not only benefit the stars financially, it would also be a way of keeping them in school.

Under the *College Sports* plan, a player who signs with an agent would forfeit his scholarship. He would remain on the roster and still count toward the school's scholarship limit, but the school could now use that money to benefit either a non-rev-enue sport athlete or the general student body. That athlete, then, would have to pay his own way through school, an oblig-ation that would be the responsibility of the agent.

If agents are looking for immediate return on their invest-ments, the NCAA should allow athletes to participate in endorsements — as long as the endorsements don't conflict with the university's commitments to corporate sponsors like Nike or Adidas. If nothing else, this plan would eliminate the financial crises that push an athlete out the door prematurely.

But while unscrupulous agents are a definite problem, at least there are some methods of governance. Unfortunately, there are no rules to control financial managers from influenc-ing kids regarding their choice of college. Eddie Fogler of South Carolina felt strong enough about it that he went public at the 1998 SEC media day, claiming that during the previous sum-mer, one former conference player had put together a ten-day trip to Europe that benefited another league school.

Fogler never mentioned names, but it was obvious to everyone in the room who he was talking about. Former Kentucky player Brett Bearup, who works for Atlanta-based Pro Trust, had sponsored a trip to France in late August. The team included Florida freshman Mike Miller, two Gator recruits — including All-America guard Brett Nelson — Jonathan Bender and two other top prep prospects.

"It's all perfectly legal," Fogler said. "The question is whether it's ethical."

When reporters told Florida coach Billy Donovan what Fogler had said, Donovan snapped, calling Fogler gutless for not confronting him.

Bearup told *The State*, in Columbia, S.C., that most of the players on the trip had already made their college commitments and were advised not to discuss their choices with the ones who had not. He said he also made sure that the trip conformed to

NCAA regulations, which allow financial managers to do such things because they aren't certified agents. Then he claimed that when coaches get beat to recruits, they always want to blame a third party.

Tempers simmered, and eventually SEC commissioner Roy Kramer had to step in, giving both coaches a reprimand. Fogler's got a point, but I thought he handled it poorly. Any complaints he had should have been directed to the office of SEC commissioner Roy Kramer. I know, from my travels, that many of Fogler's peers were upset by his statements.

Billy Donovan is a workaholic. I'm not surprised that kids are going to Florida. It's a great campus. They're in a big-time conference. They play an up-tempo game kids love to play. So it doesn't surprise me that Billy's attracted blue-chip kids such as Michael Miller, Donnell Harvey and Brett Nelson.

But what I don't understand is the difference between a financial adviser and an agent. It has to be an advantage for Bearup when he provides travel for kids and gets to know them on a weeklong trip to Paris. Bearup is doing what's legal, what's in the rules.

But I find it tough to comprehend that the NCAA hasn't jumped on that more than it has. It definitely needs to take a longer look at it. And that's what Eddie was trying to achieve, to get somebody to take a look. But the implication that Billy was a beneficiary in any way because of his relationship with Brett Bearup is a slap in Billy's face. I think Billy has the ability to recruit and sell.

If agents and financial managers are a problem, boosters can be just as bad, or worse. Former Minnesota basketball coach Clem Haskins received a $30,000 truck from boosters after the Final Four in 1997. Haskins, of course, was forced out in the summer of 1999 after allegations surfaced of widespread academic fraud involving 20 current and former basketball players.

University of Minnesota president Mark Yudof wants to implement recommendations for booster club activities. Now, all booster club expenditures must be approved in advance by the university comptroller. And awards or bonuses given by boosters for specific or extraordinary achievements must be approved by the president.

As a coach, often you're excited to invite your boosters to be part of the program. When you're the little guy, you need their help because you don't have the financial wherewithal within the university. You're asking these people to donate money to different things — your Roundball Club, your luncheons, your fund-raisers. You have to do things to keep your program going. You want a new locker room? Maybe you don't have the luxury some schools have, and you can't come up with the cash in the budget. So now you've got to seek outside revenue. But you've got to be careful. If boosters get too close to the program, get to know the kids, hey, maybe they'll do some things behind your back. The coach has to be accountable.

There's a growing suspicion that some college athletes are being subsidized in some way. In many cases, we have players who are being taken care of on campus. I hate making a statement like that because I can't document it, but I feel in my heart that the biggest danger is the alumnus who befriends an athlete. We've all heard about unscrupulous boosters. A player delivers a pizza to his house and gets a $100 handshake.

But I'm talking hard-core cheating here, breaking NCAA rules. I don't think it's prevalent, but I do know this: It exists. I know there are Charlie Tunas out there, the big fish on campus, alumni who try to get close to the players. In many cases, some of the cheating takes place after a kid arrives on campus — maybe when a kid becomes familiar with someone by doing summer jobs for him. That guy wants to adopt the kid as his so-called "son" during his time at the university. He wants to take care of him.

The NCAA did an unbelievably good job when it eliminated boosters from getting involved in the recruiting process. No longer are boosters able to contact recruits, entertain them on their campus visits or speak to them on the telephone. Why open it up again?

Coaches scream and yell at kids, "Don't you take a dime." But there's always the guy out there who wants to be able to bring the superstar over to his house for a Sunday barbecue so he can mingle with his friends and say, "Look who's at my house. I got Mr. All-American." How does he get that kid? He arranges a little one-on-one and says, "This is between us. Not coach, not anyone else. When you need a little cash, some new clothes, come and see me."

Sometimes it's not even for the kid. When the NCAA hit Purdue with a two-year probation, investigators charged that a booster violated NCAA rules by arranging for former guard Porter Roberts' mother to move to Indianapolis and providing her with transportation to home games. The school contends he was not a booster and appealed the decision.

At Dayton, a university trustee admitted making two personal loans to a basketball recruit's father, in violation of NCAA rules. Clayton Mathile, chairman of the board of Iams Company, said he made the loans in the summer of 1998 to Chuck Hall, the father of 6-6 recruit Brooks Hall, so he could qualify for a home mortgage.

The loan came in July 1998 after Brooks committed to Dayton but before he signed in November. Mathile said he had no idea he was violating NCAA rules and said Chuck Hall was advised to repay the loan and did. The school, in fact, reported the incident itself after Mathile, who has a history of loaning money to locals who needed help, mentioned the loan to the athletic director. But it was a serious issue.

Look at the University of Michigan. The situation with booster Ed Martin is a mess. Federal authorities were investigating whether Martin, a retired Ford Motor Company electrician, ran an illegal numbers operation at Detroit-area Ford plants. Back on April 28, 1999, they raided his home, seizing more than $20,000 in cash, a loaded gun and suspected gambling records.

As part of the widespread investigation, the FBI was looking into whether Martin had given large amounts of cash and made loans to former Michigan basketball players dating back to the Fab Five. Federal agents supposedly have wire-tapped conversations between Martin and several former Wolverines, including Chris Webber, Louis Bullock, Robert "Tractor" Traylor and Maurice Taylor, according to a *Detroit Free Press* investigation.

Michigan officials said the FBI told them that no evidence had surfaced about gambling on Michigan games. But it's still embarrassing, and it has school officials, including president Lee Bollinger, very concerned.

Now they want to know whether Martin had any contact with Michigan players after he was banned from associating with the program in 1997. Traylor played during the 1997-98 season. Bullock played in 1998-99. Martin became a controversial figure in Michigan basketball after a 1997 *Detroit Free Press* expose revealing that several players claimed he had given them cash and loans of $50,000-$100,000. That's heavy stuff, man.

Late in the summer of 1999, the *Detroit Free Press* reported that Bullock, ignoring a school directive, stayed in contact with Martin and accepted $50,000 from him during his four-year career, which ended in 1999. Bullock took money he considered a loan backed by future pro earnings, according to people familiar with the investigation.

Michigan hired its own law firm to investigate. Although investigators couldn't confirm that any money changed hands, they did find that Martin had an unhealthy relationship with the team. He allegedly hung around star players, got free tickets from the coaching staff, often received phone calls from coaches, had access to Michigan's exclusive allotment of Final Four hotel rooms, was around on recruiting visits with Detroit prospects, and attempted to arrange for apartments and airline tickets for players and their families.

Athletic director Tom Goss has tried to clean up the mess. He fired coach Steve Fisher, who coached the national championship team in 1989, and replaced him with Brian Ellerbee, who had been an assistant at the school. Goss tightened public access to the tunnel area outside the locker room to prevent boosters from hanging out there, and he put tighter controls on coaches and players in giving out free tickets.

If the coaches knew about Martin, they've got trouble. I'd like to believe Steve Fisher and his staff had no clue that Martin was laying out that kind of cash. Coaches should see when their players' lifestyles start to change. The kinds of cars they're driving around campus, the clothes, the gold chains. That stuff has to make a coach curious, and he has to question how they're able to get the dollars that can make that happen.

Who would have guessed that a similar problem would surface at Notre Dame? Not me. But the NCAA Committee on Infractions initiated an investigation in the spring of 1999 as to whether Kimberly Dunbar's relationship with some Notre Dame football players broke a rule stating that schools and their representatives cannot provide an athlete or relative, or friends of an athlete, with a benefit not authorized by the NCAA.

Court records show that Dunbar, who was sentenced to four years in prison in 1998 after pleading guilty to embezzling more than $1.2 million from her former employer in South Bend, Ind., provided players, their families and friends with more than $35,000 in gifts and trips. However, she was scheduled to be released early, in October 1999, because she earned an associate's degree while in jail. This made her eligible for the benefits of a new state law rewarding inmates for earning educational degrees.

In June 1995, Dunbar became an athletic representative of the university when she paid $25 to join the now-disbanded Quarterback Club, which hosted luncheons on Fridays before Notre Dame home football games. How can a school control any outsider from joining an organization such as the Quarterback

Club? To immediately label that person a representative of that school just because she joined a club is ludicrous.

She developed personal relationships with several of the players. Among them was Jarvis Edison, with whom she has a child. She took Edison, teammate Allen Rossum and Rossum's girlfriend on a $10,000 trip to Las Vegas in 1997 to see the Evander Holyfield-Mike Tyson fight. She also took ex-boyfriend Derrick Mayes, a star receiver now in the NFL, to Vegas in 1995, paying for his $1,836 plane ticket and a $756 stay at the Luxor hotel, according to court documents.

Her cover story was that she got the money for this spending spree by scalping football tickets. In reality, Dunbar bought tickets from a South Bend broker at inflated prices, then resold them at a loss just to keep people from figuring out what she was really doing.

Notre Dame officials argued that the possible infractions were secondary. NCAA enforcement officials agreed, recommending that the Committee on Infractions shouldn't view the case as major. But the committee decided to review the facts. The school was nervous enough to hire the high-priced law firm of Bond, Schoeneck and King to represent it. The firm, stocked with former NCAA investigators, specializes in assisting schools under NCAA investigation. The school maintained that Dunbar provided benefits to players in "the context of personal relationships" and not as a booster.

According to a story that ran in August, 1999 in the *Chicago Tribune*, Notre Dame officials anticipated a ruling that the football program has committed a major violation of NCAA rules. The school expects the Committee on Infractions to rule that athletic department members should have done more to learn of the players' involvement with Dunbar. The NCAA penalties could be severe.

If those players took those free trips while they still had college eligibility, they should have been banned from playing and be accountable for their involvement. But to penalize the university for her actions would be totally, totally unfair.

Unfortunately, in situations like those at Florida, Michigan and Notre Dame, everybody's equally guilty — agents, boosters, and even the players — and everybody eventually pays. What started out as a game has become a business.

Some powerful boosters don't just target players. Ask Terry Bowden. Bowden, you might recall, won ten games in 1997 and coached the Auburn Tigers to the 1997 SEC championship game. Would he really resign on his own at midseason the following year after a 1-5 start? Or was he forced out after losing the support of booster Bobby Lowder, the influential Montgomery, Ala., businessman who has his name etched on the school of business building, has control of Auburn's Board of Trustees and is said to be the most powerful man in the state?

There is speculation that Bowden paid the price for alienating Lowder and former coach Pat Dye. You may recall that Dye was forced to resign in 1992 after an NCAA investigation into allegations that safety Eric Ramsey was receiving money from a booster got the school a two-year probation. You'd never know Dye was on the outs —he still maintains an office on campus, has a half-hour radio show and seems more popular than ever.

Lowder originally was one of Bowden's backers, helping him get hired in the first place, but he apparently soured on him. Perhaps he felt he had created a monster after Bowden won his first 20 games, flexed his ego, then told Lowder, who expressed his opinion about the program a year in, that his daddy told him never to take advice from outside parties. Dye was still upset that Bowden did not give him enough credit for laying the foundation for Auburn's 11-0 season in 1993. Lowder denies he forced Bowden out. But there is no question he has pull.

According to a story in *ESPN The Magazine*, when Governor Fob James, one of Lowder's political opponents, tried to get him replaced on the board of trustees after his term expired, Lowder went out and put family money behind Lt. Gov.

Don Siegelman in the 1998 gubernatorial race. Siegelman won the election — and Lowder was back on the board.

The *Auburn Plainsman*, the student weekly newspaper, thought Lowder would play a major role in finding yet another football coach. The *Plainsman* carried a cartoon of Lowder with his arms cradled around the campus and the rest of the trustees shackled in chains and muzzled in the background.

"It took something major to happen for people to realize how much power Mr. Lowder has," *Plainsman* reporter David Ching said.

Auburn tried to wipe out Bowden's memory, redoing 16 pages in the game program. But it figures to be haunted by the Bowden family. When Auburn cancelled its football game against Florida State for the 1999 season —it was to be a historic father-son match-up — the Seminoles and the ACC were steamed.

The situation at Auburn is a sad commentary on collegiate athletics. How can a school allow an alumnus to step in and have that kind of power? How could Terry Bowden be fired, based on his record? Certainly Auburn-Florida State would have been a great match-up.

All this because Auburn wasn't happy with the progress of the team? Are you kidding me? Check out Bowden's numbers. It's incredible what the guy did. Now he goes to the world of television, where he'll be on our network at ABC-TV. And he'll go undefeated. Terry, you get the last laugh, you're now coaching at Walt Disney University.

I was hoping and praying the gambling scandals of the 1950's and 1960's were dead. Then, I started reading in the last two years about guys like former Arizona State guard Stevin "Hedake" Smith and former Notre Dame kicker Kevin Pendergast. Photo 3-1. facing page (Courtesy of *Arizona Republic*).

3

Games and Gambling

*Gambling scandals have been in college sports
since the '50's, and the ease with which
games can be fixed is mind-boggling*

When I was an undergraduate student at Seton Hall-
Paterson in the early '60's, the main campus in South Orange

had two great college basketball players, Art Hicks and Hank Gunter. I used to drive up from Elmwood Park all the time to see them play, and man, that place was rockin'. Guys I used to idolize played up there, and coach Honey Russell—who had a beautiful dome like yours truly— was the pride of the local area.

There I was, rooting for those guys, screaming and yelling —hard to believe, eh? — hoping they would win because I was so enthralled with their abilities. I later found out they were allegedly shaving points.

The news simply crushed me. I cried like a baby. I'm out there cheering these guys on, and to find out they're out there setting up games was mind-boggling. It was heartbreaking, and the papers turned it into a soap opera. It was crushing because I loved the game so much and I didn't want to see anything hurt it.

Gamblers invented the point spread in the '40's, specifically for basketball. Up to that point, bettors could only get odds on a game, and so they lost interest. The point spread was the equalizer. As a result, basketball became the most heavily bet sport in America.

But some gamblers wanted an edge, so certain college players found themselves being approached by guys with cash in their pockets. The players weren't being asked to lose, they were simply asked to win by less. "Hey, your team can still win, and you can still be a hero." Money. Win. Hero. Didn't sound so bad.

For a while, this was New York City's little secret. But it ended with a horrific thud. During the summer of 1950, Ed Gard, a senior at Long Island University — a former star whose eligibility had run out — was working in a Catskills resort when he met Salvatore T. Sollazzo, a jewelry manufacturer and gambler. Sollazzo felt that Gard, who knew all the players at LIU and many of the better players on other local college teams, would be the perfect contact guy. If Gard could line up players to throw games, he could share in the take.

Apparently Sollazzo was a shrewd judge of character. Gard went straight to the top, approaching players on the City College of New York "Cinderella" team, which had won both the NIT and the NCAA Tournaments in 1950 under coach Nat Holman. Gard dangled the bait, and three CCNY players bit. In February 1951, Ed Roman, Al Roth and Ed Warner, all neighborhood kids from the Bronx, were arrested and admitted to accepting sums of up to $1,500 to shave points in three Madison Square Garden games during the 1950-51 season. City was favored against Missouri, Arizona and Boston College and lost to all three schools.

But it would get worse. During the district attorney's investigation, it was discovered that four other key players — Floyd Layne, Irwin Dambrot, Norm Mager and Herb Cohen — also admitted to taking bribes. When the cops caught up with them and arrested them in Penn Station, it was the beginning of the end for most programs in that town. Sherman White from LIU, the best player in the country at that time, was also indicted and wound up serving almost nine months.

Those schools never recovered. The New York City Board of Higher Education also conducted an investigation and reported that the high school records of 14 players had been changed to make them eligible for admission to CCNY. The board said City could no longer play games in the Garden.

Sollazzo was convicted on 27 counts of bribery and one on conspiracy and sentenced to a term of six to 16 years in the state penitentiary. Gard had spent ten weeks in prison before Sollazzo's trial. He later pleaded guilty, cooperated with the authorities and received an indefinite sentence of up to three years, minus time served. Roth and Roman got six months each, and Roth's sentence was suspended when he joined the Armed Forces.

I know how much it hurt New York basketball. It took a long time for the city to recover. These were all city kids. They once had made the people in their neighborhoods proud like you couldn't believe, and they let it all slip away because of a temptation. It's just a shame that those players sold themselves out for a lousy few dollars. They did so much damage to the rest of their lives by having that black mark on their resumes.

Those kids weren't alone in the spotlight for long. Six months later, after Kentucky coach Adolph Rupp had said, "Gamblers couldn't reach my boys with a ten-foot pole," scandal hit Kentucky.

Three former stars — Ralph Beard, Alex Groza and Dale Barnstable — admitted to accepting $700 bribes each to shave points in the 1949 NIT at Madison Square Garden. Groza and Beard were suspended from pro basketball. A year later, Groza, Beard and Barnstable were banned from all sports for three years.

Kentucky was hit again in 1952 when big Bill Spivey, the Wildcats' All-America center, was barred from sports at the university for point shaving. Kentucky cancelled its 1952-53 season, but eventually life got back to normal in Lexington. Kentucky won the NCAA Tournament again in 1958.

You know what I find very sad? Fifty years later, this stuff is still happening. Pathetic how history keeps repeating itself. Check these out:

1961: The NCAA forces St. Joseph's of Philadelphia to relinquish its third-place finish in the NCAA Tournament because three players were allegedly involved with a gambler.

1962: Thirty-seven players from 22 schools, including Seton Hall, are implicated in a major gambling scandal that results in the arrest and conviction of three gamblers charged with fixing games.

1978-79: Reputed organized crime figure Henry Hill and New York gambler Richard "The Fixer" Perry mastermind a scheme to fix several Boston College games with players Ernie Cobb, Rick Kuhn and Jim Sweeney.

Kuhn, the only player convicted, does two and a half years in prison for conspiring to commit sports bribery and interstate gambling.

1984: Four starters on Tulane's basketball team, including John "Hot Rod" Williams, and one sub are accused of shaving points in two games. Two of the five — Clyde Eads and Jon Johnson — are granted immunity for testifying that the others also shaved points in exchange for cash and cocaine. Williams is acquitted, and none of the players do jail time, but the school shuts down the program until the 1989-90 season.

1989: Four Florida football players, including star quarterback Shane Matthews, who was a red-shirt freshman at the time, are suspended for betting on football games.

1992: Nineteen University of Maine athletes from the football and baseball teams are suspended for their participation in a gambling operation said to be worth as much as $10,000 a week. That same year, four Bryant College basketball players, who had built up $54,000 in gambling debts, are suspended, and a former player and student are arrested and charged with racketeering and gambling charges.

1995: Five Maryland athletes, including the starting quarterback on the football team, are suspended for gambling on sports. They were betting $25 or less on football parlay cards in which they attempted to predict the outcome of games. They didn't think of it as gambling because there was no bookie involved.

1996: Thirteen members of the Boston College football team are suspended for betting on college football, pro football and baseball games. Two of those suspended allegedly bet against their own team.

1997: An investigation into alleged point shaving at Fresno State starts after the team beats the point spread in fewer than one-third of its games during a 30-game span.

1998: A Cal-State Fullerton student, Jack Oh, is charged with point shaving after being accused of offering $1,000 to a player on the basketball team to throw a game against Pacific.

And these are just the instances we know about. The NCAA knows student gambling is a major problem. In fact, NCAA president Cedric Dempsey went so far as to label it "the most insidious problem we have in college athletics." He says every school has student bookies with ties to organized crime families. Duke's Mike Krzyzewski has called it a "bomb ready to explode" and says it could happen anywhere.

It could and it did. It exploded at Northwestern. That's right, Northwestern, one of the best academic schools in the country, one that I'd put on a par with Notre Dame, Stanford, Duke or any of the Ivy League schools. If it can happen at a school like Northwestern, it can happen anywhere.

Two days before the 1998 Final Four, federal indictments charged Kenneth Dion Lee and Dewey Williams, two starters on the 1994-95 team, with fixing three basketball games that season. In a separate indictment, a former Northwestern football player, Brian Ballarini, was accused of running a bookmaking operation on campus and allegedly helped players place bets. One report said Ballarini regularly took bets from athletes.

Northwestern isn't exactly a perennial NCAA Tournament team, so no one batted an eyelash when that particular team finished 5-22 under the former coach Ricky Byrdsong. But no one in the NCAA was surprised that its players were involved in gambling.

Dempsey thinks gambling is as big an addiction as alcohol on college campuses. Lee was the perfect target for gamblers. He had a gambling habit and had been threatened by a bookie for not paying his debts. Only weeks earlier, he had come off a six-game suspension for betting on non-Northwestern football games. So he listened to what Kevin Pendergast had to say.

I got to know Pendergast, a former Notre Dame place-kicker, when he was in college. He was a clean-cut kid. Once he spoke at a Quarterback Club luncheon I attended and let me tell you, the kid had the gift of gab. He had everyone rolling in the aisles. He would have been the last guy I would have thought would be involved. If it can happen to a kid like Kevin, it can happen to anybody.

Pendergast admitted to the University of Wisconsin football team recently that he placed his first bet when he was a college sophomore. As his debts mounted, Pendergast started accepting credit card offers and was using up to six cards to get gambling money. Pendergast bet on football. Then he started placing daily bets on basketball. He admitted using drugs and drinking a fair amount. He left Notre Dame with huge debts. Not long after, he met Lee and started talking about fixing games.

Lee's first assignment was to make sure Northwestern would lose to Wisconsin by more than the $13^{1/2}$ point spread in a February 15 basketball game. Lee jumped at the chance and recruited two other players —Williams and sub Michael Purdy — to make sure the fix worked. No one knows how Wisconsin covered that first night. The Badgers had a terrible first half, and Northwestern actually had a 28-21 lead before Wisconsin rallied. Lee ended up with nine points, three below his average. Williams scored nine points, slightly above his season average.

As soon as the game ended, Pendergast was back on the phone, talking to Lee, lining up the next fix, a week later against Penn State. The Nittany Lions were favored by 14 points. This time, it was never in doubt as Penn State won by 30. Lee scored just two points in 26 minutes. Williams had four, and Purdy went scoreless. Pendergast paid Lee $4,000, and Lee split the take with Williams and Purdy, prosecutors said.

As bad as Northwestern was that year, the next fix, against Michigan on March 1, was harder to pull off because the line was $25^{1/2}$ points. Lee tried to beg off but Pendergast insisted, and his partner, co-defendant Brian Irving, offered to raise the ante because the two had put more than $20,000 on the game. They lost when Northwestern covered the spread.

The U.S. attorney's office discovered the alleged point shaving during an ongoing investigation that was prompted by Northwestern's own internal investigation. In November 1998, Lee and Williams were sentenced to prison terms of one month. Only a week later, four Northwestern football players — Dennis Lundy, Christopher Gamble, Michael Senters and Gregory Gill — were accused of lying to a federal grand jury after they denied betting on Northwestern games in 1994. The indictments alleged that the defendants placed bets with Brian Ballarini, a teammate who was cooperating with the investigation.

Eventually, the truth came out. Lundy admitted he intentionally fumbled near the goal line in a 1994 game with Iowa to protect a $400 bet he had made against his team. Lundy also admitted lying to a federal grand jury investigating gambling at Northwestern when he denied he had bet on the games. He pleaded guilty to one count of perjury in a U.S. district court. He also said he bet on Northwestern games against Notre Dame and Ohio State.

It was the first time it was proven that someone had shaved points in a college football game. For years people believed it would be next to impossible to fix a college football game because of the number of players involved. That myth has been shattered. Under federal guidelines, Lundy faced six months to a year in prison, but prosecutors agreed to less time as part of a plea bargain. He was sentenced to one month in prison and two years' probation.

Lundy must cooperate with authorities and speak to college athletes about the dangers of gambling. Any time you can go out and get people to talk about what's happened in their lives — the drug scene, the alcohol scene — it helps. Perhaps if more athletes knew of the humiliation and hurt that such actions wreak on others, future problems could be avoided.

Perhaps even the nightmare at Arizona State involving star basketball players Stevin "Hedake" Smith and Isaac Burton might not have happened. Benny Silman, a 28-year-old former Arizona State student who masterminded the point-shaving scheme, convinced Smith, Arizona State's third all-time leading scorer in basketball, to fix four games in the 1993-94 season. He paid Smith $20,000 and in turn agreed to wipe out Smith's reported $10,000 gambling debt. Smith then recruited his teammate, Isaac Burton, as part of the scheme. Burton was paid $4,300 for helping fix two games.

Bettors with the inside information bet on four Arizona State games in Vegas between December 1993 and March 1994. Three were fixed successfully, prosecutors said. But the bettors lost all their money in the final game of the scheme, against Washington, when the Sun Devils beat the spread. The plan unraveled after the lines in Vegas went haywire.

Smith and Burton pled guilty, as did Vincent Basso and Joseph Gagliano, Jr., a Phoenix investment adviser, and a pair of bookies from the Midwest—Dominic Mangiamele, 61, of Mt. Prospect, Ill., and his son Joseph, 37, of Arlington Heights, Ill. They allegedly placed more than 61 bets on the games worth $501,000.

Burton was sentenced by U.S. District Judge Robert C. Broomfield to two months in jail, six months of home detention and three years' probation. He also was fined $8,000 and will have to complete 200 hours of community service.

It could have been worse if the judge hadn't been moved by Burton's heartfelt apology. But Judge Broomfield tried to send a strong message to gamblers. He gave Silman a 46-month sentence for rigging and gambling on the outcome of several Arizona State games in the 1994 season when he was an undergraduate.

Gagliano was sentenced to 15 months in prison and 100 hours of community service and was fined $6,000. Joseph Mangiamele was sentenced to three months in jail, eight months of home detention and four years' probation. He'll also have to pay a $5,000 fine and complete 100 hours of community service.

Dominic Mangiamele, Joseph's father and a former Chicago trucking executive, was sentenced to three years' probation, which includes four months' home detention, a $5,000 fine and 100 hours of community service. Basso was sentenced to $1^{1/2}$ years in prison, $27,000 in fines — the money he made off the Arizona State-USC game — and three years' parole. Smith was still awaiting sentencing.

Fixing a game is one of the most deplorable acts I can think of in athletics. Think of all that sweat and pain your team goes through to excel, then someone purposely takes a bad shot, purposely throws the ball away. That's crushing. When you put on the sneakers, the first commandment is Thou Shalt Compete. How weak are you when you're out there and hustling the buck at the expense of all the people who believe in you, trust you and are cheering for you? You let down your family and yourself. That's as disgraceful as it gets.

Gambling is an addiction. Look at Art Schlichter, the former Ohio State superstar and NFL quarterback. Schlichter got so sucked in it ruined his life. Schlichter, who has been in legal trouble since 1983, gambled away the $350,000 signing bonus the Baltimore Colts paid when they made him the No. 4 pick in the draft.

He once gambled away $300,000 in a week. He pawned his wife's wedding ring. It's a sickness that has to be treated. Unfortunately, some guys allow it to become a way of life, gambling on every little thing. Schlichter's ex-wife, Mitzi, went on tour to tell of the horrors she witnessed as her ex-husband spiraled out of control.

Schlichter was sentenced to at least four years in an Indiana prison after his fifth criminal conviction. Prosecutors estimate he stole about $800,000 to feed his addiction. He also had convictions for theft, forgery and fraud. Schlichter finally got out of prison in September, but it didn't take long for him to get in trouble. He now faces charges that last November he used pay phones at the Correctional Facility near Pendleton, Ind., to place bets on football and hockey games with a Las Vegas bookmaker.

It's so sad. Mitzi Schlichter is now director of consumer services for Trimeridian Inc., an Indianapolis-based company that offers treatment for compulsive gamblers. I just hope her message gets out to college kids in time.

In early 1999, there were reports the FBI was looking into allegations of point shaving at UCLA after the Bruins lost their final two football games to Miami and Wisconsin. Sources in Los Angeles told the *New York Daily News* and the *Los Angeles Times* that the probe most likely was started after UCLA players were seen with a reputed member of New York's underworld on several occasions in a Long Beach restaurant.

The FBI interviewed several players but was unable to uncover any evidence. The school was eventually exonerated, but All-America quarterback Cade McNown, a first-round pick in the 1999 NFL draft by the Bears, reportedly was told by the FBI to stop associating with shady characters.

You just hope people want to do things the right way. But you've always got the rotten apple out there that wants to destroy the barrel. My feelings are simple. If any athlete is found guilty, he definitely should do jail time. You're affecting people's lives and hurting a lot of people. Of course, feeding this gambling misery is the fact that sports gambling is big business.

I have to applaud the valiant efforts of Mitzi Schlichter who has devoted herself to helping the misfortunate that are clinically addicted to gambling. Photo 3-2. (courtesy *Indianapolis Star*).

Bookmakers in Nevada, the only place in the country where sports betting is legal, reported that $80 million was wagered on the 1998 NCAA men's basketball tournament. That's more than the Super Bowl! The FBI estimates that close to $2.5 billion is wagered illegally on the NCAA Tournament every year, including such things as office pools. Nevada state law doesn't allow betting on games involving in-state teams. But during the NBA lockout, I heard there was increased betting on college games. Hey, people seem to want the action.

Gambling is a major concern. The NCAA has been try-ing to educate students that gambling has become a part of campus life, how you've got to be careful as an athlete to make sure you don't get involved because you feel obligated. The NCAA has its own five-part plan:

- Each school needs to conduct comprehensive gambling education programs that target all students. These programs need to discuss the dangers of sports gambling and provide help to those in need.

- Congress needs to put through legislation that would prohibit gambling on the Web and would require Internet providers to block access or discontinue service to gambling Web sites.

- Sports-handicapping services need to be exam-ined more closely. Many sports handicappers advertise their success in picking winners with no evidence to support their claims. Without some kind of regulation, consumer fraud prac-tices will continue.

- More studies need to be done on teenage and college-student gambling to get a better under-standing of how big it is on campuses and of student attitudes toward gambling.

- There has to be continued assistance from law enforcement.

The NCAA considers gambling such a serious problem that it was part of the agenda of the 1999 Division I Working Group to Study Basketball Issues. In its report, the panel called for increased sanctions against gambling. Its recommendations:

- Athletes who bet on college or pro sports through organized gambling should be suspended for a year and lose one year of eligibility.

- Second offenders should lose all eligibility.

- Athletes who attempt to fix a game or bet on a game involving their own institution should lose all remaining eligibility.

I buy that entirely. There's no question that if you play that fixing game with your own school, you shouldn't be a part of the college environment.

Times have changed. Years ago, when I was starting out in coaching, it was all about getting to the gym and teaching X's and O's, talking to kids about classes. Today it's so different. Coaches have to worry about their kids hanging out in a local club with some bad dudes who try to get some inside information about the team so they can go out and lay a bet.

Bill Saum, director of agent and gambling activities for the NCAA, has testified in Congress about the problem. Some of the statistics he noted were brutal. Saum pointed to a 1996 NCAA-sponsored survey of 2,000 male student-athletes in Division I football and basketball — chosen at random — conducted by the University of Cincinnati. It showed that more than 25.5 percent had gambled on college sports events other than their own while they were in college. Almost 4 percent admitted to gambling on games in which they played. Worse yet, three of the athletes actually admitted receiving money from a gambler in exchange for altering the outcome of a game.

A University of Michigan study on student-athlete gambling that same year was equally upsetting. The school sent out questionnaires to 3,000 football and men's basketball players and got 758 responses. More than five percent wrote they had either given inside information to gamblers, bet on games in which they played or shaved points. Saum claimed illegal gambling occurs on virtually every college campus.

Sports Illustrated did an excellent series on the problem back in 1995. Saum quoted a passage from one of the stories: "On most campuses, illegal sports gambling is seldom more than a conversation away. Somebody in the dorm knows a bookie. Somebody in the fraternity knows a bookie. Somebody in the frat is a bookie."

If you don't want to believe the figures, believe your eyes. The CBS news magazine "*Public Eye*" followed up the *SI* piece by airing film from a college bar on game day — just a few blocks from a Division I-A school's football stadium. A hidden camera showed student bookies on cell phones accepting bets on college games.

"If I had to design a place to groom gamblers, I would design a college," said Patrick Collins, the assistant U.S. attorney who prosecuted the Northwestern case. He was speaking at a gambling awareness seminar hosted by Northern Illinois. "College students have access to credit cards, access to athletes and access to computers."

Students at Columbia University put those facts into practice. In 1998, New York police uncovered a gambling ring in Queens involving a student named Joseph Della Pietra, a former member of Columbia's baseball team who lived in a fraternity with 18 varsity athletes. Pietra's ring allegedly accepted bets on the phone from fellow students, and Pietra would then phone in the bets to the bookie. Sometimes the ring took 2,000 bets a week and allegedly did $10 million in business a year.

The bookies must have been everywhere in Chestnut Hill in the fall of 1996. Boston College suspended 13 football players for gambling, including two who bet against their own school the previous month in a game against Syracuse. Thomas Reilly, the Middlesex County D.A., said the two players — Marcus Bembry and Jamall Anderson — did not influence the outcome of the game, which Syracuse won, 45-17. But it was enough to eventually get them tossed off the team for good.

"I will not, and the team will not, accept back to the program anybody who has bet against Boston College," BC coach Dan Henning said.

The other 11 players involved were suspended for the rest of the season. After reports about the betting started filtering in, odds-makers in Vegas initially took BC's game against Notre Dame off the board. But they resumed taking bets by the end of the week, listing Notre Dame as a 22- to 24-point favorite but circling the game, which meant sports books would take only half of their usual bets.

If the NCAA had its way, there would be a ban on betting on college sports events altogether. "We believe the game should be watched for spontaneous action and reaction on the field, not for the point spread," Saum said. He also called for all media outlets to stop publishing point spreads on college games.

I too wish they wouldn't publish that information. Theoretically, I'd like to see the NCAA limit access to its Tournament only to those papers that don't print the daily line. But then you get into a First Amendment, freedom of speech thing.

The NCAA's statements were in response to a report issued by the National Gambling Impact Study Commission, which conducted a two-year study. The NCAA had three other recommendations in the report:

- a national minimum gambling age of 21,

- a continued ban on Internet gambling,

• and harsh penalties for underage gambling.

In addition, the FBI and the NCAA spoke to each of the Final Four teams and officials in both San Antonio and St. Petersburg during the Tournaments in 1998 and 1999. Each participating student-athlete received a security card that included telephone numbers for assistance should he be approached.

NCAA athletes and college athletic officials are already prohibited from betting on college or pro sports. But there's nothing to prohibit somebody from going to a casino. In fact, the same organization that blasts gambling doesn't seem to be too concerned that the Western Athletic Conference held its conference tournament in Vegas from 1996 to 1999 and housed the majority of teams in casino hotels, just a quick elevator ride away from the slots and the dice. Utah coach Rick Majerus, for one, was not a happy camper knowing his team would be exposed to that environment.

Even more absurd, the college athletic directors have held their annual convention in Reno and accredited the Las Vegas Bowl, which pitted San Diego State against North Carolina in December 1998. And the NCAA was forced to wipe some egg off its face on the eve of the 1999 Final Four in St. Pete when someone informed it that CBS-SportsLine, which is associated with CBS-TV, the very same network that has put out more than $2 billion in rights fees to air the Tournament through 2002, was offering gambling services online.

I know the NCAA is watching and listening, though. I once received a phone call from the NCAA's Saum because I had been a guest on a radio talk show that took gambling ads. I knew nothing about that. But Saum was concerned, told me if the producer called again to think about it. I told him I would. I won't go on those kinds of shows.

That's what I like about Larry Donald's *Basketball Times*. There are no gambling ads in there. I don't want to be associated with gambling in any way, shape or form. I was very upset a couple of years ago when my preseason magazine came out and there on the back page was this huge advertisement for Players Club, a tout service.

I went wacky, yelling and screaming. I called the publisher to make sure to write a letter to ESPN, every conference and the major media members, telling them I had no knowledge of what was done. The ad had been accepted without my approval. I told the publisher I would not be involved with the magazine any longer if ads like that continued to be accepted. The magazine no longer accepts gambling ads of any kind.

One way the NCAA is keeping its eye on game fixing is by asking for the help of the very people from whom they'd like to pull business, odds-makers and sports books. The NCAA actually used the betting line service from Vegas odds-maker Roxy Roxborough in the Tournament, keeping a watchful eye on betting patterns. A swing of a couple of points in a day would catch its eye. The NCAA's computer program is the same one the big casinos have. It allows the NCAA to monitor the point spreads at all the different casinos and all the games.

In addition, Saum has sent a memo to all college coaches, athletic directors, trainers and sports information directors containing a list of 47 publications and 67 individuals with whom they are not to have any conversations. Those publications and people, called "touts," peddle information advising their clients on how to bet on games. These individuals and their publications argue that they're only in the information business and depend on the games being clean to survive. But it's clear the NCAA isn't of the same opinion.

The NCAA is looking into all aspects of college athletics. According to a comment made by Indiana's Bob Knight during a TV interview with ESPN's Digger Phelps, the NCAA might need to keep an eye on its own officials as well.

"You and I have always thought that the most susceptible guy in any gambling scheme is an official, without any question," Knight said. "I mean, if we only knew the truth about games that were controlled by officials having gambling interests, I think it would be amazing."

I talked to Bob about that statement. He said he didn't necessarily mean to take a shot at the officials. He was making a general statement. I think he'd actually like to take that statement back. I think what he was trying to comment on was the control a referee has in a game. I haven't seen anything that would indicate to me that we have officials going out there trying to fix games. I've never seen an official I can point to and say that guy is on the take.

Knight's statement really upset Hank Nichols, the national coordinator for men's basketball officials. Nichols said if you make a statement like that, you've got to back it up with specific games, specific situations you're aware of. To indict all is not fair.

Today, these officials are such stars themselves. Some get more airtime than David Letterman. I guess anything is possible. In every profession, you find some weakness. But the NCAA must be taking some of Knight's comments to heart. Cedric Dempsey has said that background checks for the officials selected to work the Division I men's and women's basketball tournaments will be initiated in 2000.

Dempsey stressed that the move is part of a continuing effort to fight gambling influences and was not based on any specific suspicions. Dempsey says it's unclear whether outside investigators or in-house personnel would be used to conduct the background checks. The NCAA has jurisdiction only over the 96 officials who work the postseason Tournament. Conferences control officials during the regular season.

"I don't want to go into another Tournament without it," Saum says. "Anybody associated with the game is at risk."

Saum says Nichols approved of the background checks. I think what you've got to do is educate everybody to the evils of gambling. Kids, coaches, officials, trainers, it doesn't matter. The NCAA has tried to do that. It's sending out a lot of educational materials and videotapes. It's trying to enlighten athletes by bringing in people to talk to the kids about the scandals of the past, about how lives have been destroyed.

In the end, it gets down to one magical word, whether the issue is drugs, gambling or alcohol...character. It's that simple. What kind of person are you? Are you in it for yourself or for your team?

The NCAA can legislate all it wants, but it comes back to character. I hope we're not on the verge of a major epidemic. Once a sport loses its credibility, it becomes a laughingstock. This is the fifth decade of point shaving, and it doesn't look like it's going away. You'd think kids would learn. But you're always going to have an element of society that wants to take shortcuts that will sell people out for their own gain. They see cash, cash, cash and figure out a way to get it.

The NCAA is trying, but more needs to happen, and fast. I know coaches work hard, talking to their players, bringing in enforcement people to speak to their players about staying away from certain places, certain characters. But until we legislate gambling out of the arena and employ the recommendations made above, it's just a matter of time until another school, maybe your alma mater, makes front-page news for fixing a game.

And if it didn't make you sick to read about Northwestern, Boston College and Arizona State, believe me, you'll feel it then.

I hope NBA commissioner David Stern is serious about instituting an age minimum for college players to enter the NBA. Photo 4-1. facing page (AP Photo).

Chapter

4

Show Me the Money

The financial success of the NCAA Tournament
now needs to trickle down to the players
or the Tournament will disintegrate

If the American dream can be measured in dollars, then the NCAA men's basketball tournament is the U.S. mint, baby. The most successful college event ever, it has quickly become an equal to the ever-powerful Super Bowl for marketing dollars and fan frenzy.

CBS has broadcast the Tournament since 1982. In 1995, with three years remaining on its old deal, it penned an eight-year contract that pays the NCAA $1.73 billion for broadcast rights through 2002 because the network had no "right-to-match" clause and didn't want to lose one of its biggest properties in open bidding. That translated to $215 million for the rights fee for the 1998-99 season alone. The deal also includes airing championships for other NCAA sports.

But in 1999, because ISL, ABC-ESPN and Fox all wanted to compete with CBS for the Tournament, speculation was that a new deal might reach $4 billion for ten years, according to Jim Wheeler, vice president of ISL Worldwide, a Swiss marketing firm that holds the rights to soccer's World Cup for both men and women. Wheeler told Rudy Martzke of *USA Today* that the $4 billion figure would include TV rights, Internet, licensing, marketing and sponsorship.

CBS and Host Communications had serious discussions about presenting a combined offer for marketing and licensing while enabling the NCAA to deliver live video and audio coverage of its other championships over the Internet. Sources estimate the network would have to shell out $3.5 billion to get the deal done.

I'm not surprised by it, but the numbers have blown my mind. Now you can understand why CBS paid such a huge price and was doing everything it could to hold onto the property. It's a great event. It captures the imagination of America. It is the greatest three-week period in sports. For all the flaws people want to find, come next March people everywhere will be talking about nothing else. Why? Simple. As former Big East commissioner Dave Gavitt said, college basketball is great because it's all about the name on the front of the game jersey, while the NBA is about the name on the back.

Even with all the underclassmen defecting early, March Madness is always special and electrifying. Sure I'm disappointed about not being able to see some of the superstars who left early such as Allen Iverson and Ron Mercer, but every year it's still a thrill watching teams play their hearts out for the schools they represent.

The NCAA should be excited too. The association generated $275.9 million in revenue last year from men's hoops. As a non-profit organization, it distributed $148 million to Division I major colleges. Aside from the TV money, the NCAA generated $17.1 million from ticket sales.

The Final Four alone generated $3.6 million in ticket sales, $350,000 from merchandise and millions more with sponsorships from giant corporations like Pepsi, GTE and Nike. Each of those sponsors paid between $1 million and $4 million to use the Final Four name in its TV commercials, print ads and contests, according to the *St. Petersburg Times*.

Interest in men's basketball is at an all-time high. We've come a long way, baby, since 1939, when the NCAA Tournament started. In the beginning, the NCAA Tournament didn't have the same clout as the National Invitational Tournament (NIT), which had started the year before and was attracting big-name coaches, big-name teams and big crowds to New York City's Madison Square Garden, which became the Mecca of college hoops.

The first NCAA Tournament was won by Oregon, but nobody really noticed. Only 5,500 fans showed up at Northwestern's Patton Gym in Evanston, Ill., to watch Oregon defeat Ohio State, 46-33, in the finals of an eight-team tournament. When the receipts were counted, the ledger showed a $2,531 loss. Teams in the '40's were lucky to walk away with a $100 profit after travel expenses. The unbeaten 1956 University of San Francisco champions, with Bill Russell and K.C. Jones, netted $12,000.

The Tournament absolutely exploded following the Magic Johnson-Larry Bird showdown at Salt Lake City in

1979. Three years later, in 1982, a bidding war broke out as CBS and NBC battled for the TV rights. The field expanded to 64 teams in 1985, and the rest is hoops history. It's been a win-win proposition for TV, the NCAA, the schools, the coaches and the players who get to market themselves for the pros.

Amazingly, college football looks to be 60 years behind in coming around to the fact that a postseason tournament, an expanded playoff, would be good for the sport, generating as much if not more revenue for Division I-A schools.

In 1998, ISL came up with a proposal for a 16-team major-college NCAA playoff to begin in 2003, two years after the current Bowl Championship Series (BCS) contract runs out. The plan would pay the major schools $300 million over eight years — about double what the Bowl Coalition disperses now.

The first-round and quarterfinal games would be played in early December at the site of the higher-ranked team. The semifinals and title game would use three of the four current Bowl Championship Series sites; the Fiesta Bowl, the Rose Bowl, the Sugar Bowl and the Orange Bowl, with the title game set for the week before the NFL Super Bowl.

The numbers are awesome, and they apparently have caught the attention of Bobby Bowden of Florida State and Philip Fulmer of Tennessee, the two coaches who played in the first Bowl Coalition Series championship game in 1999. Both coaches were happy the BCS worked out for them, but they would like college football to take that next step.

"It's progress, but my personal feeling is there should be a playoff at some point," Fulmer said right after the match-up was decided. "Obviously, things worked out this year. But we had an 11-1 team four years ago and were left out of the alliance. We played Ohio State in the Citrus Bowl and finished No. 2 in the country, but we weren't in the mix because of an early loss to Florida."

"I had a feeling we were closer to a playoff than ever before because there were too many scenarios as to who would play in the big game in the last two weeks of the season," Bowden said. "Things worked out for us, but there were several other teams that deserve to be there as much as we do. I was never a proponent of a playoff before, but I think we ought to have a four-team playoff."

But SEC commissioner Roy Kramer, who came up with the idea of the BCS in the first place, thinks the current system is fine. He says the BCS had three goals in its first year:

- Enhance the regular season,
- match the consensus No. 1 and 2 teams in a bowl game; and
- find ways to maintain the health of the overall bowl system.

He believes it met these goals. "I'm not here to say there will never be a college football playoff," he said. "But I don't believe it will be run by someone in Switzerland."

Kramer claims that even after the BCS contract runs out, the Pac-10 and Big Ten have a contract with the Rose Bowl for three more years, ending in 2005, and without all the major conferences lined up, you can't sell a playoff. He's also concerned that the timing wouldn't work because first-round games would be played on college campuses while the NFL season is still being played.

But what he harps on most is that a playoff, he feels, could hurt the integrity of the regular season and destroy the traditional late-season rivalries such as Ohio State-Michigan, Florida State-Florida and USC-Notre Dame. Kramer says he doesn't want college football to turn into college basketball, where March Madness has become the big thing.

"The NCAA Tournament is everything to college basketball," he says. "People don't care about December and January."

But there's nothing like a national championship game in any sport. I say, bring on December Delirium. College football teams currently play 11 games during the regular season, 12 if you play in a conference that has a playoff.

The saddest thing in football is if a team has one little slip, one little slip in the regular season, you're practically eliminated from the chase of the dream, the chase to be No. 1. That's unfortunate. It makes people think about scheduling. Why should you go out and schedule all the great ones? Take a Notre Dame vs. Michigan season-opening game. An early loss kills you and practically ruins any national title hopes.

Some schools, like Kansas State in the late '90's, have tried to avoid playing big non-conference games, effectively avoiding an early loss in order to climb the polls. But the strength of schedule issue eventually catches up to you, as it did the Wildcats in '98. That's the biggest difference between college basketball and college football. In college basketball, there are 64 teams in the NCAA Tournament. You have to win six games to win the championship.

In football, the two teams making it to the BCS championship game are selected with help from a computer and two subjective opinion polls. I'd like to see a 16-team football playoff, with the bowls hosting the games. It would take three weeks in December and you'd work to a climax on New Year's Day. Seed the teams accordingly, that would be major, major, major. Then, if I'm a school like Notre Dame, I'm not worried about playing a Michigan in the opener because one loss doesn't necessarily knock you out of the running. And I don't want to hear about players missing class, that's Christmas break.

The concern over eating into study time reminds me of something Bobby Knight complains about all the time, the late starts on ESPN. He and I have battled about that on several occasions. I always tease him and say, " Come on, General, give me a break. How much studying is going on at those hours?"

While ESPN owns the regular season, the road to the NCAA final four goes through CBS's studios. And, in 2000 the venue will be the RCA Dome in Indianapolis. Photo 4-2. (courtesy *Indianapolis Star*).

Kids plan their schedules accordingly. It's not like ESPN is asking the same teams to do this every week. Sure, if it's a steady diet, then I agree it's too much. But the kid who wants to get through college is going to get through. Today, with the tutoring and study halls and all the support available, an athlete has to really mess up not to get his degree.

The hunt to be No. 1 does have its drawbacks, of course. At certain schools that have become accustomed to winning, anything but first place is greeted with disbelief. I had a Duke basketball fan come up to me recently and say,"Oh, man, I'm disappointed about last year." And I just looked at him and said, "What? Duke was 37-2." Yet at Duke, the stakes are different; same goes for other great basketball schools like North Carolina, Indiana, Kentucky, Kansas and UCLA.

It's no longer about just getting to the NCAA Tournament, it's about winning it all. In football you've got schools like Michigan, Notre Dame, Nebraska, Florida State and Florida that have tasted success and continue to do so. And, the football programs face the same problem; "What have you done for me lately?"

Take Ohio State in 1998. The Buckeyes were a great team, but on one Saturday they had a breakdown, stumbling in the final four minutes at home against Michigan State. Well, Michigan State beat the Buckeyes, and Ohio State — which might have been the best team in America and likely would have been the national champion — never got a chance to play for the title. A playoff would fix that.

Coaches at these "Fortune 500" schools are like CEOs. Texas A&M just gave its football coach, R.C Slocum, who took his team to the Big 12 championship, a seven-year deal worth $7 million. Slocum was given an annual raise of $220,000, with a boost in base salary from $185,000 to $300,000.

Other earnings come from radio and TV money, a housing allowance, cars, a country club membership and a shoe contract. Slocum is the winningest coach in Texas A&M history. In his ten seasons, A&M has played in eight bowl games, five on New Year's Day, and finished in the top 20 nine times.

He's not the only one. Phil Fulmer of Tennessee signed a six-year, $1 million per year deal right after the Vols won the national title. Steve Spurrier of Florida is making almost $2 million annually. To lure Rick Neuheisel away from Colorado, the University of Washington offered him $1 million per year, guaranteed over the next five years, and offered to help him pay off an $800,000 home loan Colorado gave him. In basketball, guys like Mike Krzyzewski and Rick Majerus of Utah reportedly have deals that pay them close to $1 million a year.

I have a lot of people come up to me and say, "It's absurd what these coaches are making. It's ludicrous." But I think the guys who have proven that they pack arenas, graduate kids and bring in the big bucks deserve to make the mega dollars.

USA Today ran a story on Jimmy Valvano — God rest his soul — a few years after he won the national title in 1983 and estimated his salary at between $500,000-$600,000 for being the coach and athletic director at N.C. State. An ESPN producer asked me to get his reaction to that story. So there I am, showing him a graphic and saying, "Jimmy, look at the numbers. For coaching basketball and being an AD? Is that real?"

He said, "Dick, are you serious? That was five years ago." He laughed about it, but as we went off the air I knew that the statement would upset many folks in the academic world. You better believe a majority of professors don't want to hear about a coach making that kind of cash. But as he told me so often, he was like a CEO. He was an entrepreneur in terms of the money he was bringing into the university through marketing and sponsorship deals.

The same can be said of Rick Pitino who was "Mr. Entrepreneur" when he was at Kentucky. And believe me, special charismatic guys like Pitino and Valvano deserve the big bucks.

Campus Chaos

The professors at these universities certainly deserve more money than they're making, but teachers are not under the same type of pressure coaches are under. A teacher knows whether he or she has done a good job in dealing with those kids in class.

Tell me Tubby Smith doesn't have a little pressure walking the streets of Lexington if Kentucky loses to Tennessee in a big SEC game the night before. The newspapers, the radio talk shows. Are you telling me the talk shows are talking about professors? I can guarantee you it's, "Tubby Smith—he played his son, Saul, too much. What is he doing out there?" Fans don't know what the English professor did nor do they care. Everybody's an expert...everybody's a genius.

Things have changed drastically with coaches today. There's much more pressure than 25 years ago when I was coaching in college, because back then we didn't have the kind of media scrutiny we have now. If something goes wrong in your program today, it's all over the news — ESPN, CNN, MSNBC — by that afternoon. People are learning about it nationwide.

When I was coaching, I had the local beat writer following me around and that was it. At the University of Detroit, we were never on national TV other than an NCAA Tournament game we played against Michigan in the Sweet 16. And with that scrutiny comes the additional stress of the job. Every coach today, high school, college or pro, puts a certain amount of pressure on himself. He has a sense of pride, and he knows his success or failure is based on winning and losing.

I remember going to church a couple weeks after I was fired by the Detroit Pistons back in 1979. I saw people who used to hit me up for tickets or autographed basketballs from some of my Pistons players such as Bob Lanier and M.L. Carr. I had been their best friend. But all of a sudden, since I'd gotten fired, it was like I had a rare disease. I specifically remember going up to one guy and saying, "Hey, man, I was good enough to get you tickets. You can't say hello to me? I'm still Dick Vitale." But the guy wanted me to say, "Dick Vitale of the Pistons." And I felt ashamed.

I was very hurt for all the people who believed in me when I was with the Pistons. They came out with a campaign, with banners, all kinds of bumper stickers — "Re-Vitalized." When we didn't win, it was an embarrassment. I was constantly reminded about that. Guys on the air saying, "Hey, you're supposed to be Re-Vitalized. You got Re-Vitalized all right, blown out by 30."

The most intense pressure comes from within, and it beats you down. If you've reached the NBA level, chances are you've been successful in order to get there. In college, high school, it's a little different. When I was at the University of Detroit, the school was not exactly drawing huge crowds. After a while, we had some success and were fortunate enough to create some enthusiasm. So from that standpoint, everything was Utopia.

When you're coaching, you're either way up or way down. Those who can withstand the pressure and succeed realize the rewards. And baby, make no mistake the rewards are high. We're talking mega, mega dollars. And let's face it, successful coaches are a key part of any school's financial success. Tell me John Thompson wasn't a giant financially at Georgetown over the years during the Patrick Ewing and Alonzo Mourning eras in terms of the Georgetown paraphernalia the school was able to sell.

But coaching isn't as easy as simply drawing out plays. What makes a good coach? The criteria are different on every level. The current trend in the NBA is to hire ex-players, like Doc Rivers, Gar Heard, Larry Bird — guys who really know about how to deal with that athlete, guys who know about travel and life in the limelight.

In college, it's a whole different ballgame. If I'm hiring on the collegiate level, I'd look for three things:

- The ability to sell. Can he go out and get us the type of players it takes for our program to be able to compete with the giants? If you can't recruit, you can't succeed. These guys on the other sideline are no dummies. X's and O's? Everybody gets a little taste of those. At clinics across America, you can learn about the 2-3 match-up and the 3-2. But I'd want a guy who can sell, market and promote the program. Everything is relative. At Kentucky, for example, recruiting is a different world for Tubby Smith than it was when he was coaching at Tulsa. At Tulsa, you're not recruiting the McDonald's All-American. At Kentucky, it's a necessity, where Tubby is going up against the Dukes, North Carolinas and UCLAs.

- The ability to be able to motivate and inspire, to blend egos. If I'm at Duke, I'd better have the ability to take five McDonald's All-Americans and make them understand their roles. I'd better be able to take a Shane Battier, who was a Mr. Basketball in the state of Michigan, and convince him we need his defense and rebounding more than his scoring, get him to understand that, with Elton Brand, Trajan Langdon and William Avery, he may be a fourth option. Motivation is more than coming out and playing with rah-rah spirit. It's the ability to motivate an athlete to give up a little of himself to be part of a winning program.

- The ability to handle the technical aspects of practices and games. I'd make that No. 3 because most guys have that. Most guys don't get to the Division I level without understanding when to call a timeout, how to set up practice drills.

People say to me, "Dick, you must be eating your heart out, you're not coaching." I always tell people, "I coach every day on TV and I haven't lost a game in 20 years." It's a lot easier in that TV tube than on the sidelines.

People say, "Dick, you never jump on coaches." Well, look at the games I do. I do games featuring the best of the best. Carolina-Duke. What am I screaming about? How am I going to bury Hall of Famers? I'm not sitting there doing games with 5-25 guys.

TV obviously has a lot of power. It has the ability to arrange prime match-ups and promote certain programs because of their name recognition. Big-name schools have always paid lesser-known non-conference opponents to play them on TV, provided the smaller school is willing to take a road trip.

But the one thing TV can't dictate is who's going to be that national champ. I try to sell what I see. If I see somebody producing and I see somebody I believe in, I promote him with a passion —anything I've ever attacked, I've attacked with passion. When I get behind somebody and feel he's gotten a raw deal, like Fran Fraschilla did at St. John's, I'm not afraid to speak my mind.

Guys accuse me of constantly singing the praises of Duke. Well, what is there not to like? You go there and it has everything you dream about in college basketball. Guys play hard. They go to class. They do things the right way. They have discipline. They go out and win. The crowd is behind them. So it's really easy to sing their praises.

Because I do so many big games, what I say gets printed more. But I never go into a game saying I'm going to build up this guy. People say I'm building up Quin Snyder and Tommy Amaker because they're from Duke. But I've been to their practices and these guys have ability. I can see it, and I try to tell people what I see.

Campus Chaos

The NCAA Tournament and the TV coverage it generates is really responsible for the successes of the College of Charlestons, the Gonzagas and the Valparaisos. Many athletes across the United States can tune in and see action from all over.

Kids are saying, "You know what, if I go there, I can fit in. I'll still get some TV exposure." It's a great recruiting tool as TV exposure of this quality plays a vital role in building winning programs. Remember, recruiting is the backbone of any program.

Jimmy Harrick of Georgia suggested at the SEC summer meetings that the last few NCAA Final Fours were like watching JV basketball. He went on to say that the last good teams were Kentucky in 1996 and UCLA in 1995. Sorry, Jimmy, I've got to disagree with you big-time. The 1999 final between Duke and Connecticut was brilliant basketball. It was competitive, pitting the two best teams in the country in a championship setting.

I had picked Duke to win in a close game, and Richard Hamilton let me know about it afterward. He was waving his trophy and saying, "Hey, Dicky V, Dicky V, you picked us No. 1 in your preseason magazine, but you got off the bandwagon. You went with the Dukies." He's right. I had picked UConn preseason No. 1, Duke No. 2, but I really felt Duke was going to win it all once the tourney started.

But the special thing about the NCAA Tournament is that the Goliaths of the college basketball world can no longer avoid the Davids the way they do in the regular season. The big guy can't run from the little guy in March. Southwest Missouri State in 1998 pulverized Tennessee. Who would have thought a team like Southwest could go against a program like Tennessee, an SEC team with all the dollars behind it, and beat them by 30, beat them like a drum? That's because a Steve Alford can sell his team at Southwest Missouri State the idea of being part of the folklore of the Tournament.

90

The success of the little guy creates coaching stars who eventually move up the ladder the way Steve did when he moved on to Iowa. Everybody wants a piece of the pie. They see the success of a College of Charleston, the success of a Coppin State, a Gonzaga. So now schools are saying, "If we go Division I, sign three good players and get a little lucky, all of a sudden we're part of the Big Dance."

The stakes aren't the same for a Coppin State and a Gonzaga as they are for a Duke or a Kansas or a Kentucky. For those Cinderella teams who get in the Tournament, it's an unbelievable reward. Win a game or two and it becomes a monster. Gonzaga went down to the wire with Connecticut in the regional finals. It was right there, banging on the door with a chance to go to the Final Four.

Schools like Stony Brook see that and have to think twice. People are out there trying to emulate them, and as long as they feel they have a chance, why not go Division I? It's that magical word...Dollars. Schools are seeing what's happening.

The one thing that scares me about that is the college presidents are saying to their guys on the sidelines, "Hey, look what John Kresse is doing down at Charleston, look what Ron "Fang" Mitchell is doing at Coppin, look what Don Monson did at Gonzaga and Homer Drew did out at Valparaiso. Why can't we get a piece of that pie?"

So now they're putting pressure on the coach at the mid-major and low-major level to win big. If he doesn't win big and get to the Big Dance, he's a failure and you find his name on the transaction pages in March and April. Pack the bags. That is sad.

Presidents and academic types have a right to be aware of what's happening at their schools. But the decisions should be made by athletic administrators who are involved in the process on a daily basis. A basketball coach wouldn't tell a psychology prof how to draw up a curriculum for his class.

There's nothing wrong with some give and take. I think a president should meet with his coaches on a regular basis, get a little feedback on what's going on in athletics. But the AD should be allowed to make the final decision. The problem is, a lot of athletic directors don't have the power.

What happened down in Auburn in football was a shame. No way Terry Bowden should have been fighting for his job because of one bad year after the numbers he put together. But a lot of powerful alums and boosters got involved. We need more ADs like C.M. Newton down at Kentucky. He's in charge. He's the man. But schools all want instant gratification because it boosts enrollment and alumni donations big time. They're writing checks when the team is winning.

I've been getting letters from Gonzaga fans. I never got a letter from a Gonzaga fan. Ever. They were upset about having to play Temple in the Great Eight. They wanted a rematch against UConn.

If those fans are upset about that, just imagine what will happen if the athletes ever hold out for a piece of the pie. Murray Sperber, a professor at Indiana who wrote a book called *College Sports Inc.*, which examines the big business aspect of NCAA sports, thinks it's just a matter of time before star athletes sue for part of the profits.

There's even been one idea thrown out there by former Duke guard Dick DiVenzio, who would like to unionize the players. I can't see that happening. Some things should be changed, but I don't think it has to be a rebellious situation, where you're creating animosity and chaos between the athletes and the schools.

NCAA president Cedric Dempsey has done a superb job since taking over the top job in 1993. One of his strengths is the fact that he has a real feel for what the NCAA is all about thanks to his diverse background in intercollegiate sports, which includes stints as athletic director at Houston and Arizona. He claims players will never be in that situation because there's already precedent in the courts affirming that these are students and thus will never get paid. Never say never.

The NCAA has talked about allowing student-athletes to hold jobs during the school year that would pay them up to $2,000 a year. It would supposedly create a healthy environment for all. Forget about it. It's pure nonsense. In my mind, the negatives outweigh the positives for the few dollars that could be earned by an athlete.

In the revenue-producing sports like football and basketball, many of the athletes who are admitted to school carry some risk academically. They need more time than ever in terms of tutoring, guidance and direction. And when does a basketball player, participating in a sport that spans two semesters, have time to work and take care of his studies?

Now you've got coaches who have to become an employment agency, placing players in jobs. You'd have one player moaning and groaning, "Hey, how come he has a job delivering pizza, working three hours a day? He's delivering pizza and getting great tips. Me, I'm busting my gut."

I think Charlie Ward had it right. In 1993, Ward, now a guard in the NBA, was quarterbacking Florida State's national championship team and was on his way to winning the Heisman Trophy. He made national news when he was publicly critical of university officials for making money off him by selling replicas of his jersey with his number on it. And how much did Charlie receive from this? Nothing. Zippo.

No wonder athletes in sports such as football and basketball are angry. They figure since they're making money for the university, why shouldn't they get something back in return. There are a lot of people out there —including myself — who agree with Charlie, who say, "Well, wait a minute now. These kids who make all of this happen, when do they get a piece of that pie?"

The argument against that is, quite logically, "Well, they get a scholarship, they get a free education." Let me tell you something, the average non-athletic scholarship student who goes to school has the flexibility to work, to participate in a business, to get a little professional training. The athlete doesn't have the time between the academics and playing in that arena or stadium to do the things a normal student does. That's why I've said for years that athletes should be rewarded with more than just the opportunity of getting a scholarship. They should get some spending money, maybe $150 a month to buy pizzas, whatever.

Obviously, what I look at is the revenue coming in from major basketball programs and football programs supporting all the other programs, and I think, in those cases, those athletes deserve something. There are some programs in place today, such as the Pell Plan, which awards grants to students most in need. But it's not enough.

Here's my plan to ease the pain. Young players could be evaluated by a committee of people who have been around the game and who can analyze players and make guesses as to who will be future first-round draft choices. These students would be allowed to borrow $50,000 per year from the NCAA, which they have to pay back when they ultimately become pros. I think that would help kids realize, "Hey, I can stay in school, and with this cash I can help my family out and get some of the things I need."

These are special kids who, if they stay in school, will mean a lot to the university in terms of fund-raising and marketing the school because of the excitement they generate. Any athlete who is on scholarship in a revenue-producing sport — football, basketball and women's basketball if it's making money for the school — should get a minimum of $150 a month in spending money to be able to do the things the normal student does. Years ago, they got $15 a month. It was called laundry money.

Include a couple of airline tickets as part of the scholarship. Why do they need them and why shouldn't other sports be included? Let me explain. My two daughters were scholarship athletes at Notre Dame. They played on the tennis team. Their argument to me is, "Wait a minute, we put in as much time as any football player or basketball player and we deserve a stipend if they're going to get one." But the problem is the cost factor. That tennis program didn't add to the school's coffers.

Now here's my other point about a stipend for athletes in revenue-generating sports. I'll focus on basketball because that's what I have experience in. Let's take Johnny. He enrolls in September, and the first thing he's doing is weight training. He's going to physical conditioning program sessions with the coaches, which is now permitted before the start of practice.

Then comes the season. It's intense like you can't believe from October through March. It spans two semesters. Now comes the postseason. Want to beat out that incoming freshman next year? Better play in the summer league. The point is, where is the time for these kids to work a job? There is no time. They've got to handle the academics as well as the pressures of athletics.

And the airline ticket thing bugs me. I know coaches who have gotten calls from new recruits just before they're supposed to report to school saying, "Hey, coach, nobody sent me my airline ticket. How do I get to school?" The coach says, "Sorry, son, we can't do that. Your scholarship includes only room, board, tuition and books. We're not allowed to pay for your transportation."

Why not allow the kid two trips, one round-trip ticket from home to campus and then back at the beginning and end of the academic year, and the other during the course of the year to visit his family. Sometimes a kid is recruited from California to play in Connecticut or somewhere else in the

East, and he comes from a situation at home where it's tough to come up with cash for long-distance airfare.

The reality is success breeds success, and those responsible for success deserve to be compensated. Coaches are. Networks are. Schools are. The kids deserve to be as well. The sooner we accept the fact that this is a business and work toward an equitable arrangement for all involved, the sooner we can get past the hypocrisy that runs rampant through the system.

The death of one of my former players, Les Cason, really shook me up. He was a high school star who never realized his true potential because he started running with the wrong crowd. Photo 5-1. facing page (courtesy of *The Bergen Evening Record*)

Chapter
5

Being the Man

*The game isn't just X's and O's anymore, now
society's problems are every coach's problem*

Man, did I cry on April 21, 1997. That was the day I
received a call from pastor George Ibach of the Bowery

Mission Ministries in New York City calling to notify me of the passing of one of my former players, Les Cason. Les, who was 43, died of complications of AIDS at a Manhattan nursing home.

Who was Les Cason? Let me simply say that I would never have had all the beautiful things that have happened to me professionally if I had not met the big kid. Les was a 6-9 center who played for me when I was coaching at East Rutherford High in north Jersey. He opened a lot of doors for me, took me to two state championships. He was a high school All-American and a PTPer. He scored 2,871 points, which is still the all-time Bergen County record, and he had a world of potential.

Things changed dramatically during his senior year. Even though we were going unbeaten and dominating the action, he wasn't the same player. He no longer played with the same passion for the game and his skills seemed to be diminishing.

I was worried about him, but anytime I would question him about his actions off the court and about the people he was hanging out with, he would get defensive. When I confronted him about being involved perhaps with the wrong crowd and making bad decisions off the court, he would simply snap back at me and say stuff like, "That's just what my buddies are saying, that you're using me to further your career." Man, did that hurt, because I remember working so hard with Les as a youngster to the point that I became obsessed with wanting to see him be the best.

I remember how embarrassing it was when Les was selected to play in Sonny Vaccaro's Dapper Dan Classic featuring the best high school players in America and he was totally outclassed. I then challenged him about possibly being involved in drugs and he denied it, saying I didn't trust him anymore. Well, I hoped and prayed that I was wrong, but my suspicions were later proven true. I spent hour after hour trying to help him.

After a while, I started asking myself, "How do I reach him?"

I felt like a failure. I didn't fulfill my responsibility as a coach. I was guilty, as are so many others, of turning my back when he made mistakes. I was guilty of getting him back into the lineup, of always finding a way to make sure he was eligible.

Would it have been better had I told him, "That's it, Les, no more basketball in your life"? At the time, I felt basketball was the only thing he did well and that if I took that away from him he'd have nothing left. I don't think he would have graduated high school.

But there were some people in the academic world who thought I should have severed ties. They may have been right. But he always found a way to remain eligible. At the time, my argument was, do you penalize the whole team because of his immaturity? I wanted to win, and this kid was a key part of winning.

Sometimes it's hard to know the right thing to do. I was hoping and praying that through basketball, I could motivate this young guy who had a world of potential. But I couldn't.

And he really had talent. Today, you hear about these 6-9 guys handling the rock on the perimeter and everyone goes "Wow." But Les was doing that 25 years ago. He came along in New Jersey basketball during the same time as Brian Taylor, who went on to Princeton, and John Shumate, who went on to Notre Dame, and believe me, Les was everything they were.

Willis Reed loved him. Reed was the captain of the New York Knicks at the time. I thought Willis could reach him. He was a great role model, the Karl Malone of his time. So I got him involved. Willis saw Les at a camp and said he was one of the best 6-9 players he'd ever seen in terms of mobility and agility.

Willis and I had become friends when he and I ran a benefit basketball game in Clifton, N.J., called "The Sammy Davis Classic," for a youngster who lost both his legs and his right arm in a train accident. Willis helped bring in some of the biggest names in the NBA to play and all the money went to the Sammy Davis Foundation.

They don't come any better than Willis Reed; he's a real humanitarian. But Les wouldn't even listen to him. I had arranged for Willis to meet Les, but Les blew him off a couple of times. Les became a real problem.

I thought he was headed for greatness in college. Everybody recruited him. Schools called and said, "Maybe you can come too." Initially, I entertained the thought. But in the end, I said, "No way. Under no conditions."

Les really hurt me one day when he said that I was just another white guy using him to advance his own career. That really blew me away because I had poured my heart and soul into trying to make Les a better player and person. Color has never played a part in my decisions. The comment made me furious.

I told him, "Where were all these so-called friends of yours when you were just a no-name kid on the street? All of a sudden they're your best friends." I told him that there was no way I was going in any package to any school with him. I told him I was going to make it on my own because I had enthusiasm, spirit and a lot of fight in my body. That's when I got the opportunity to become an assistant at Rutgers, and things turned out well for me.

Les signed with Long Beach State and Jerry Tarkanian. But Les' grades had dipped in his senior year of high school and he had to go to San Jacinto Junior College, the same school that produced Ray Williams, who starred at Minnesota and Walter Berry, who became "Mr. Basketball" at St. John's.

The coach there called me on numerous occasions to tell me Les wasn't living up to the standards they wanted. Les kept calling me for help, so I helped him transfer to Livingston College of Rutgers University, where he played for Tom Young, but he never realized his potential. He never became the force we all knew he could be. It was sad.

One of the hardest things for me to deal with is that Les is no longer with us. Les should be retired today, a multimillionaire, living like a king.

From Rutgers, he bounced around on the streets and got involved with drugs. Les became part of the Washington Square Park scene in New York City where he was arrested a number of times and became addicted to drugs. I continued to get letters from him in which he told me how desperate things were. His only family was his mom, Mary Johnson, who was very ill at the time. He was just hanging out in a park in the Bowery, doing nothing.

I wrote him and told him that I would love to help him but that I would forward cash to Pastor Ibach and ask him to handle the money for anything Les needed. Les wrote me back and claimed I didn't trust him, that I never believed him. He asked why I was giving the money to the pastor. He claimed the pastor was only trying to take advantage of him. I may be naïve, but I'm not that naïve. Anyone could have figured out that Les would just pour that money back into his veins.

One day I received a phone call from Ian O'Connor of the *New York Daily News* who was writing a story about the 1996 NCAA championships that were being held at the Meadowlands in East Rutherford, N.J. But the focus of his story wasn't going to be about Kentucky or Syracuse. His story was focusing on how ironic it was that 25 years earlier yours truly had led East Rutherford High to a state title with a star named Les Cason, and how our two lives had gone in different directions.

There I was, Ian wrote, sitting there on top of the basketball world, talking about the game I love on TV, while Les was walking the streets of the Bowery peddling drugs. Ian told me that I would be relieved to know that Les told him he wished he'd only listened to me about making quality decisions in his life. He told me that Les took full responsibility for his situation and blamed no one but the man in the mirror.

So many times in sports, an athlete blames everyone but himself. But Les was man enough to acknowledge that he was responsible for his own troubles. It's hard for me to sing his praises when he violated everything I believe in.

Every time I talk to youngsters and parents I speak about the perils of the alcohol and drug scene. I've made many a mistake in my life, but I'm proud to say that drugs and alcohol have not been one of them. You don't need those artificial highs.

But in the world of sports, sometimes selfishness overcomes you. The hunger to win blinds your better judgment. I know, looking back, that I did the right thing for Les. We truly thought we could use the game to motivate him academically, but obviously it didn't work.

Today's college coaches are dealing with the same problems. But unfortunately, some are crossing the line between helpful tutoring and having others actually do the class work for the athlete. Take for example, Clem Haskins, the Coach of the Year in 1997 after taking Minnesota to the NCAA Final Four, who stepped down in the summer of 1999. His program allegedly was rife with academic fraud.

Minnesota chose to buy out his contract, for $1.5 million, even though NCAA investigators found no evidence implicating him. University president Mark Yudof said it was "extremely likely" the fraud did occur and that a change was necessary to restore confidence.

"I didn't fire Clem," said Yudof, "I didn't ask him to resign. He is leaving by mutual agreement. But I held more cards than he did because the contract allows his termination without cause."

102

Minnesota coach Clem Haskins tasted plenty of success with the Gophers, including this NIT title in 1998 and a Final Four berth in 1997. But unfortunately, no one kept an eye on the players homework. And, Haskins was forced out after allegations of academic fraud. Photo 5-2. (AP Photo).

Haskins had three years to go on a ten-year contract. He was 240-165 in 13 seasons. But he had been under pressure ever since March 1999, when the *St. Paul Pioneer Press* broke a story just one day before the Gophers' first-round NCAA Tournament game with Gonzaga. A former tutor and office manager in the academic counseling unit, Jan Gangelhoff, claimed to have written more than 400 papers for 20 Gophers players from 1993 to 1998.

She had proof, showing the *Pioneer Press* computer files that contained more than 225 samples of work. The newspaper printed eight of those papers on its Web site. Now all are available. Gangelhoff claimed some of the first papers she wrote were edited by Alonzo Newby, the program's academic counselor, and former assistant coach Milton Barnes.

"He [Barnes] wanted me to rewrite it more like something the player would write," Gangelhoff said.

Gangelhoff said she often had several players turn in the same papers for different classes, or she would use excerpts from one paper in another, and she went on to allege that Haskins paid her $3,000 and that Newby was the go-between. Newby, who refused to meet with investigators, eventually was fired for refusing to cooperate. Newby refused to be interviewed by the *Pioneer Press*. Barnes, now the head coach at Eastern Michigan, said he didn't know anything about it.

Gangelhoff did say she never was asked by a member of the coaching staff to do course work, but she considered it compensation when the school took her on two road trips, including one to Hawaii in 1995. The *Pioneer Press* eventually gathered evidence that Haskins paid $1,050 by personal check for that Hawaii trip.

The warning signs were out there. Elayne Donahue, the retired director of academic counseling-intercollegiate athletics, found out that an assistant coach was driving players to Gangelhoff's house in the spring semester of 1998, at a time when she was no longer approved to tutor. Donahue passed the information along to athletic department administrators, but the information was ignored.

At the time Gangelhoff, who now works for a casino in Wisconsin, left the school, she never intended to reveal she had done the work. But she became angry when the school self-reported one incident of academic fraud and linked it to her. Athletic director Mark Dienhart wrote Gangelhoff a letter disassociating her from the program, even though she had already left the school. She said she decided then and there that something had to be done.

The *Pioneer Press* also reported that, according to last year's NCAA statistics tracking recruits between 1983 and 1991, Minnesota has the lowest graduation rate of any Big Ten basketball program. Not good for a program involved in its third major scandal in the last three decades. Since the original allegations, there have been accusations of improper payments, travel irregularities and improper relationships between the team and university police investigating crimes involving players. Specifically;

- Christine Shevchuk, the ex-girlfriend of former player Courtney James, told NCAA investigators that James said he was given cash by Haskins, received new clothes from assistant coaches and cash for an airline ticket, The *Star Tribune* reported. She said that after one home game, James told her he had some things to take care of and would meet her in her dorm room. Later, James walked in with a business-size envelope containing cash. He told her Haskins gave it to him, reportedly as a reward for playing a good game. Shevchuk told investigators from the University of Minnesota, who were investigating possible NCAA infractions, about conversations she had with James regarding coaches allegedly buying him a suit at the Mall of America so he would be well-dressed for games. Shevchuk also claimed that an assistant coach gave James cash at the Minneapolis-St. Paul airport to pay for a trip home to Indianapolis during the 1995-96 season.

• Shevchuk sought a protective court order during their eight-month relationship in which James allegedly hit and threatened her. Haskins and some coaches visited the family and told them Shevchuk should have sought his help instead. Shevchuk's father secretly recorded the conversation.

• Another player, Russ Archambault, also contends he took money from Haskins. Archambault told investigators Haskins gave him cash "eight to ten times."

• A former student tutor, Rebecca Fabunmi, told The *Star Tribune* that McKinley Boston, the vice president for student development and athletics, tried to get her to change her story when she complained about a football player who allegedly masturbated under a table during a tutoring session. When the player continued to harass her, she said, she reported the problem to a university detective, who talked with athletic officials but never filed a report. Boston claimed the incident was handled in an appropriate matter.

• Several other women have since accused the university of intervening in assault and criminal sexual conduct investigations involving seven football and basketball players between 1993 and 1997.

The University of Minnesota finally released a massive report in July 1999, produced under the supervision of Minneapolis attorney, Don Lewis, that painted a gruesome picture of the way the athletic department handled these types of cases. The report didn't name names but cited several incidences in which the school was completely out of bounds.

In one particular case, where a female student told police she wanted to press charges against a football player who allegedly assaulted her, an assistant coach spoke with the woman, convincing her not to pursue it. It was the fifth allegation of assault or sexual misconduct involving that player within nine months, and his coaches had been aware he had been accused of sexual misconduct when they recruited him.

In the wake of that report, the university announced some long-overdue policy changes. Athletes are now automatically suspended from team play if arrested or charged with sexual or domestic abuse. Sexual abuse allegations are to be referred to the Office of Equal Opportunity and Affirmative Action and cannot be resolved informally unless approved by the school's general counsel. Men's athletic officials can no longer contact victims or participate in interviews of victims, witnesses or alleged perpetrators unless approved by investigators and individuals being interviewed.

From the start, Haskins claimed he was innocent. When the story broke and the four players allegedly involved — Miles Tarver, Antoine Broxsie, Jason Stanford and Kevin Clark — were suspended for the Gophers' NCAA game with Gonzaga, pro wrestler-turned-governor Jesse Ventura claimed the *Pioneer Press* stories were sensationalistic and offered his own solution. "Why not let kids go to college and just be athletes when they're there?" he told *Sports Illustrated.* "No classes. Let them simply play."

Man, let's hope he didn't mean that. I mean, that's totally wacky. There are a lot of athletes out there who bring more than just jump shots to the table. I know a lot of athletes who have gone on to become successful doctors, lawyers and politicians. Does the name Bill Bradley ring a bell?

The incident at Minnesota is frightening. Why is it you've got to beg and plead for a kid to go to class? That's one of the risks of recruiting and signing kids who are risks academically. We had that even back when I was coaching. But we all like to think that when we put kids in our environment under our guidance, we can turn them around.

Clem Haskins always poured his heart and soul into the job. But a coach has to be held accountable and responsible for everything that happens in his program. Coaches can't just sit and take the praise and stand in the winner's circle and get all the praise and the long-term contracts and not expect to take heat when something bad happens.

Every good program in America has a coach who follows up on players and what they're doing in the classroom; he contacts the teachers to make sure the athletes are turning in their papers. But there's a feeling out there that a coach should not get too involved with a faculty member.

Sometimes a coach will send somebody from the athletic department who's been a go-between with the academic side. But as soon as you do that, you open yourself up to unbelievable scrutiny because the implication is you're looking to get a favor. Many in the academic world think an athlete should be treated like any other student, just let the kid do his work and get his grade.

But there's nothing wrong with a coach showing concern for a player's academics, showing he truly cares. Nobody showed more concern than John Thompson of Georgetown. He was crazy about making sure his players went to class and got their papers in on time.

But in the Minnesota case, somebody crossed the line. Sometimes there might be an academic advisor who thinks, "You know what? I want to look good in the eyes of the coach. So I'm going to take care of these players and take care of them in more ways than just tutoring them. I'll actually do the papers for them and help them get the grades. Now I'm rewarded by that coach for doing a blue-chip job."

To me that's wrong. My only problem with Jan Gangelhoff is that she waited so long to come out with these accusations. Why wasn't she complaining to the administration from day one, saying, "Hey, man, this coach is trying to get me to do a paper. I'm here to give some academic counseling. I'm not here to do the actual paper"? Or why didn't she go right to Clem Haskins and complain? But she didn't do that, so she's not innocent either.

Still, there's no way that cheating should exist on a college campus. Some people don't want to be in college. They're only using it as a door to the next level, to be able to play in the NBA.

I buy into the fact that every university has certain professors who love the idea that a star player is a member of their class. And human feelings can enter into it. Sometimes a player gets special attention because his name is in the paper. Are some teachers going to go that extra mile for an athlete? Yeah. Sometimes. Sometimes not.

At some schools, tutors help athletes get to class, help them with papers, help them study for tests. To me, that's too much of a good thing. I'm all for group studying, but when it gets to the point where the tutors are doing the extra work, there's a problem. How do you legislate against that?

Ideally, every coach wants his players to be eligible, wants to see every kid graduate. But a coach knows. Some coaches, who can't recruit academically at the same level as schools like Duke, know that if they want to compete at that level athletically, they have to roll the dice, take some chances on kids, take some academic risks.

But there are some kids who just aren't ready for college. They can't communicate, can't write papers. I don't like to see athletes abused, and they are when they're not ready for college. It's painful watching them sit in a classroom unprepared. Schools are trying to help.

The University of Iowa, another Big Ten school, has established a special two-tiered academic advising system for all its athletes. In addition to the regular academic advisor, student-athletes are assigned a special academic adviser. The school hopes this will eliminate inappropriate contact between faculty and coaches.

Other schools have taken less positive steps. *Sports Illustrated* took Ohio State to task for finding a way to keep All-America linebacker Andy Katzenmoyer eligible. Katzenmoyer needed to pull his GPA up to 2.0 during two five-week summer school terms. One of them was "AIDS: What Every College Student Should Know." The other was golf.

SI obtained copies of two anonymous letters sent to school president William Kirwan. One claimed the only two grades given in a mass communications course were "A" and "*A-minus*" and questioned how Katzenmoyer could be squeezed into a golf course that had already been full. A second letter asked how Katzenmoyer could have been granted a grade change for an art education class he had failed the previous semester. Kirwan told *SI* that while the basic facts of the letters were correct, nothing was done for Katzenmoyer that couldn't be done for any other student at the university.

"Some will take the facts one way, I saw that no rules or regulations were broken," he said.

Still, in the wake of the controversy, Ohio State has tightened its academic standards. Rob Murphy, a preseason All-America guard, was suspended prior to spring ball and eventually dismissed from the university because of continuing academic shortcomings. Then, in August, the program was hit with another bombshell when three members of the Buckeyes' nationally ranked recruiting class were turned away by the school's admissions office because of academic deficiencies. The NCAA Clearinghouse declared three more, including prep All-America tackle Bryce Bishop of Miami, ineligible.

It seems that Minnesota has more problems in its future too. According to athletic director Mark Dienhart, the NCAA could place Minnesota on probation and temporarily pull two scholarships as a result of the scandal. That was enough for former Virginia coach and current AD Terry Holland to pull out after he became the leading candidate to replace Haskins.

Holland, who took the Cavaliers to the Final Four in 1984 and made nine NCAA appearances, has a reputation for being one of the most principled people in the sport. He was the chairman of the men's NCAA basketball committee and would have done a lot to clean up Minnesota's image. Minnesota reportedly offered him a seven-year contract worth $1 million a year. Holland was making $250,000 at Virginia. But he's 57 and hasn't coached in nine years. He didn't want to wait several seasons before being able to be competitive in the Big Ten.

Minnesota eventually hired Dan Monson of Gonzaga, whose team advanced to the 1999 regional finals against UConn. The contract pays him $490,000 per year for seven years, plus outside income. The school included a $25,000 bonus in Monson's contract if the team's collective grade point average exceeds 2.8 on a 4.0 scale.

But there are some major differences from Haskins' deal. For one, the contract contains a clause that holds him accountable for rules violations committed by assistant coaches and for "any university employee for whom he is administratively responsible or representative of the university's athletic interest that, in the judgment of the university, he knew or should have known about with reasonable diligence and oversight."

At one point, there was even some thought to shutting down the program for a year so they could clean up the mess. That's what Tulane did after its point-shaving scandal. But that doesn't solve anything. Any time you have a problem in school —whether you have a problem in the chemistry department, the history department —you don't close it down. Minnesota had a problem. But I think a better way is to find out the source of the problem, eliminate the problem and then go on.

Sadly, coaches these days aren't dealing only with the academic problems of their players, they also seem to be spending more time serving as guidance counselors, and in some cases probation officers.

One bizarre example of how messed up things are these days occurred at Fresno State. In 1998, Fox Sports Net paid $700,000 to Black Canyon Production, which in turn paid $50,000 in rights fees to Fresno State to get an all-access look inside its program during the 1998-98 season.

The film painted a frightening image of a program in chaos, chronicling everything from two assaults, a late-night roller car accident, eight drug suspensions, a player's admission of marijuana use, Chris Herren's three weeks in a rehab, a visit by Mike Wallace of "*60 Minutes*" and the now-infamous incident involving two players, Avondre Jones and Kenny Brunner, who were arrested for allegedly assaulting and robbing a man while armed with a Samurai sword. They both pleaded not guilty. The result? Ten Fresno State players out of a total of 12 on scholarship were suspended from the team. *Hoop Dreams* this wasn't.

Coach Jerry Tarkanian originally was hoping to paint a rosy picture of his program, but what was caught on tape was just unbelievable. I thought his players would have had a better understanding of what was happening, but some of them acted like comedians. All that piece did was paint a negative picture of what college is like.

I have to believe Tarkanian had to be upset with some of the actions of his players, especially knowing a camera was following them around. I've known the Tark for over 25 years, and I've had the pleasure of watching him in action—with his players on the court and in the office. He loves the game and he loves to work with kids who are looking for a second

Jerry Tarkanian of Fresno State always seems to be in the spotlight, whether winning big or being chased by the NCAA. Photo 5-3. (AP Photo)

chance—he's done wonders with players that no one else wants.

That's why I've dubbed him the Father Flanagan of college coaching, because he possesses a special gift to communicate with those players who need a guiding hand. Remember, it's a very special coach who is able to recruit and relate to the blue chip student-athlete. At least something positive came out of it. Fresno State has now instituted a no-nonsense code of conduct, and it now forbids the recruitment of anyone with a felony conviction.

The NCAA didn't drop the hammer on Fresno State, but that wasn't the case with Purdue. The NCAA put that Big Ten school on two years probation for major violations involving an assistant men's basketball coach and two others close to the program. The Boilermakers can still play in the postseason and appear on TV, but the committee on infractions said Purdue violated rules regarding recruiting, extra benefits and ethical conduct.

As a penalty, the school must repay up to 90 percent of revenues generated by a 1996 NCAA Tournament appearance. The school will be on two years' probation and will lose a scholarship in both the 2000-01 and 2001-02 seasons. The university will be limited to four paid recruiting visits during the next two seasons. All records from 1996 will be expunged.

Frank Kendrick, the chief focus of the investigation, received a one-year off-campus recruiting ban and was reassigned pending the outcome of the appeals. The committee penalized Purdue for a $4,000 loan that Kendrick had arranged for Luther Clay through Bank One in August 1995. The NCAA believed Clay when he said Kendrick told him he would not have to repay the money. The loan was never paid back, minimal effort was made to collect the balance, and eventually the bank charged off the loan after the player transferred to Rhode Island after a year.

The committee also found that Kendrick arranged extra benefits for former Purdue guard Porter Roberts' mother,

Angelia Allison, by Indianapolis businessman Gene McFadden, whom the NCAA described as a booster. McFadden helped Allison relocate from Chattanooga, Tenn., to Indianapolis and gave her temporary housing. He also provided her with transportation to several home games. Purdue and McFadden both deny he is a booster. McFadden said he met Roberts while dating the mother of another Purdue player and not through Kendrick. He claimed Allison worked as a housekeeper to repay the loans.

The NCAA began preliminary inquiries at the school in the summer of 1997. By that time, Purdue had already disciplined Kendrick for giving a ride to then-recruit Jamaal Davis during the dead period. Kendrick was fined an undisclosed sum and forbidden to recruit off-campus for ten days during the official recruiting period.

In December 1996, AD Morgan Burke said Kendrick and the coaching staff inadvertently violated rules by making 15 phone calls to Davis, who later signed with the school but did not play as a freshman because he was academically ineligible. He played 12 games as a sophomore before quitting the team in December 1998. Kendrick was eventually reassigned to another job at the university. Purdue is appealing.

The vicious recruiting wars create a nightmare of stress for young assistant coaches, like Kendrick, who are always striving for the slightest edge over their competitors. Many times they do what they feel are bending the NCAA rules and talk themselves into believing they are not actually breaking the rules. Unfortunately, they usually end up jeopardizing, if not outright destroying their coaching careers.

Purdue head coach Gene Keady had to have been shocked and totally dismayed upon learning of these infractions. He has always upheld the NCAA rules and has long been an active force in the fraternity of coaches serving on NCAA committees. I've known Gene Keady for over two decades and I can flat out tell you that he is a man of high principle and integrity.

I think too often coaches these days coddle these kids and break too many rules to find a way to get them into the lineup. We hear plenty of stories about the tough lives some of these players live. But there comes a time when a kid has to turn that bad hand into a good hand. A scholarship can open up a lot of doors, but I'm a believer that you've got to earn the right to wear that uniform.

I've always been behind guys who do things the right way. It would break my heart if I had to read something negative about somebody like an Alex Rodriguez or a Derek Jeter or a Nomar Garciaparra. I've gotten to know these three, and am so impressed with the way they carry themselves off the field as well as on the field.

I went to the Tampa Bay Devil Rays' game against Anaheim and told Mo Vaughn about a youngster who had cancer and was sitting next to me. He hit a home run then gave the kid his bat during the game. Wow, do I ever cheer for guys like Mo Vaughn.

But I get tired of hearing about the guy who has one alibi after another. Just because he can play, there's always somebody willing to stick his neck out and give him another chance, despite the threat of prison. I'm not saying a guy shouldn't get a second chance. Guys make mistakes, fine. But we hear about guys only after they're charged. We don't hear about all the times others have gotten them off.

At Duquesne, nine students — including three players from the basketball team - were charged in June 1999 in a federal indictment with taking part in an elaborate scheme to defraud PNC Bank of $36,000. Another suspect, who did not attend the school, Robert Unoarumhi of Philadelphia, was also named in the suit and helped orchestrate the scheme along with basketball players Simon Ogunlesi and Jamal Hunter. The scheme involved buying bankcards and unused personal checks from students, then using them to make $35,961 in fraudulent withdrawals and money orders between February 22 and April 12, 1999, prosecutors said.

116

Ogunlesi and Hunter were suspended from the university pending the outcome of the case. The personal checks were allegedly used to make phony deposits into the students' accounts. Unoarumhi then withdrew money from the inflated accounts by using the check cards at automated teller machines. He and Ogunlesi also purchased money orders using the check cards, authorities say. PNC officials soon noticed the suspicious activity and reported it to authorities. This is mind-boggling. It's too bad they didn't use their brains in the classroom. They could have been all-academics.

At UCLA, there was an uproar when 14 current and former football players, including seven starters, such as fullback Durell Price, guard Oscar Cabrera and linebacker Ryan Nece, were charged with misdemeanor counts of illegally possessing handicapped parking permits by claiming fake injuries.

The players allegedly submitted Department of Motor Vehicles applications with the signatures, addresses and medical license numbers of non-existent physicians. The permits allowed the players to park in special handicap spaces, to use metered spaces for free and to park in limited time zones indefinitely.

Nine of the athletes involved eventually pled no contest to the charges in July and apologized in court. Each was placed on 24 months' probation, ordered to pay fines, penalties and restitution, and to complete 200 hours of community service. In addition, UCLA coach Bob Toledo suspended the nine players still with the team for the first two games of the season. That did not stop disabled activists from booing the players outside court, or UCLA chancellor Albert Carnesale from ripping the players involved.

"This behavior is particularly insensitive because it was carried out by student-athletes, for they are among the most able-bodied of all," Carnesale said.

These handicapped placards would have saved the players the $132-per-semester fee for parking and allowed them to park anywhere on the crowded Westwood campus. Some people will do anything to save a buck. Or make one.

At Pitt, freshman guard Fred Primus was arrested on charges of grand theft and receiving stolen property and dismissed from the team for an incident during a road trip. The 19-year-old was charged with stealing $2,200 worth of jewelry from a home in Malvern, Pa., 25 miles west of Philadelphia. He was sent to Chester County prison on $10,000 bond. Guard Jason Boyd, who apparently had hosted some players at a friend's home in Malvern, was dismissed for violation of team rules. He was reinstated just one week later.

It's the macho effect, I guess. Too many of these kids must feel they can get away with anything, whether it be academic fraud or violence. If you're a star, then somehow, someway, they'll find a way to get you into the lineup. The pathetic thing is that no matter what the NCAA legislates to try to change that mentality, the pros are setting a terrible example by ignoring just about every misdeed and letting bad eggs play. Everybody talks about finding a guy with great character. In the meantime, teams always seem to get the guy who has good ability in the door, and out of scrapes.

Sometimes kids get involved in self-destructive behavior. At the University of Kentucky, football player Jason Watts pled guilty in May 1999 in connection with a drunken driving crash that killed two of his friends, teammate Arther Steinmetz and Eastern Kentucky student Scott Brock, on November 15, 1998. The three were on their way to go deer hunting after a night of celebrating Kentucky's win over Vanderbilt when Watts passed a car on US Highway 27 in Pulaski County and lost control of his pickup truck, which overturned.

Steinmetz, 19, was a transfer from Michigan State who was sitting out a year. Brock, 21, was a close friend of Kentucky quarterback Tim Couch. Watts suffered a lacerated arm and was charged with two counts of second-degree manslaughter and one of wanton endangerment after tests showed his blood-alcohol level was $1^{1/2}$ times the legal limit.

He was sentenced to serve ten years in the Pulaski Co. jail but was released after serving two months and granted probation. During his five-year probation, Watts must attend an alcohol awareness program and do 50 hours a year of community service. Watts blamed himself for the deaths.

"I literally see my buddies dying in my arms," he told students at Southern Adventist University, about 18 miles south of Chattanooga, as part of the school's drug and alcohol awareness week. One of the biggest problems on college campuses is binge drinking, drinking just to get high. And it's not just dumb kids who are doing it.

My bottom line is this. Coaches have to be responsible for the kids they recruit. I know coaches are very hurt by what happens with some of their athletes. They pour their hearts out and can't understand why a kid decides to go bad. Or makes bad decisions.

Just two weeks after Connecticut won its first NCAA Tournament on March 29, 1999, sophomore guard Khalid El-Amin was arrested by Hartford police when two detectives, acting on a tip from an informant, busted him in a north-side neighborhood. They pulled him over after he'd run a red light and found five small bags of marijuana. Teammate Rip Hamilton was also in the red Audi at the time — the car was borrowed from a school friend — but was not charged in the incident.

El-Amin offered a conditional plea of guilty to misdemeanor possession and failure to obey a traffic light after meeting with his lawyers. He was sentenced to six hours of community service and was instructed to give three speeches to middle school students about the evils of drugs.

"It was definitely hard," he admitted. "I learned not only to make better judgments but to act the way you're supposed to act. You can be on top one second and on the bottom the next."

El-Amin has since apologized to teammates, fans and family and gone on with his life, riding on a flatbed float in the Huskies' national championship parade that drew more than 200,000 fans to downtown Hartford.

"I've received letters from students from 50 schools telling me they still supported me even though I made a mistake," he said. "It's just something I want to put behind me now."

El-Amin is smart enough to realize what's at stake, and lucky enough to receive a second chance. But I like the way El-Amin and Connecticut handled it. The school didn't try to make excuses, didn't try to defend him. He was wrong in what he did, wrong in being in the wrong place, wrong with what he had on him. But Jim Calhoun confronted him, and the kid came out and apologized for hurting so many people. You could see the pain in his face. He knew he had to be a better role model. Let's hope he remembers his lesson.

The NBA is always pushing character, character, character. But you knew that guys who had major problems off the court in 1998, like Keon Clark of Vegas, Jelani McCoy of UCLA and Jason Williams of Florida, would be drafted in the first round. You could bank on it. Then the NBA people turn around and say, "Oh, he's changed." Right. I believe in giving a kid a second chance. But kids who commit felonies and assaults aren't cut out for college. That's not what it's about.

Need an example of how the pro ranks are setting a bad example? Check out Latrell Sprewell. As we all know, Sprewell was a star in the 1999 NBA playoffs for the New York Knicks, getting standing ovations from the fans in the Garden. But when he played for the Golden State Warriors making millions, he was suspended for a year for assaulting his coach, P.J. Carlesimo. He claimed Carlesimo verbally abused him.

That's right. Choked him at a practice in front of his teammates and threatened to kill him, then came back 20 minutes later and had to be dragged off by assistant coaches. For what he did, he should be in prison serving time. That was an assault on another human being. You attack somebody, you go to jail, man.

He's lucky P.J. didn't sue him. P.J. had some damages. He suffered. His coaching credibility is damaged.P.J. has a heart of gold, and I think Sprewell was very fortunate to get a second chance.

And Sprewell? After being reinstated and traded to New York, he's back in the game, making his millions. It blows my mind.

Check his background. Throughout his career, he's had problems. Maybe he's learned. But he had no right to lay a hand on anybody. If he weren't an athlete, if he were in the general work force, he would have been in serious trouble.

Sprewell's behavior must be contagious. A month or so afterward, there was a situation in an Oakland, Calif., high school in which a player hit his coach. It pains me to see that those terrible lessons do indeed trickle down to the lower grades.

You always think you can solve any situation. Every coach thinks he can be a guiding light and can change a player's attitude. But sometimes a guy has a track record, and that track record keeps going on and on. In the end it comes down to mutual respect; you communicate your feelings, they communicate theirs.

And you hope you can both get on the same road, go to the same place. If you're going to be successful, I'm going to be successful. If you do a great job, I'm going to do a great job. If you do a great job, you're going to make a lot of money and I'm going to make a lot of money. But if you start breaking that line and that bus starts going off the road, there's going to be a collision.

I could have never coached Dennis Rodman. I guess I should join the club. Rodman's out of basketball now, working for a pro wrestling circuit as a bad guy. Perfect typecasting. The Lakers had enough of him. They tossed him after he wouldn't show for practices, refused to go into games, took off for Vegas when his marriage was on the rocks. When Rodman played for the Bulls, they accepted Dennis for what he was. He'll show up for games, do what he does best — rebound and defend. Phil Jackson could live with that. The Lakers couldn't.

My initial reaction? If a player doesn't show up for practice, if he's late, doesn't go into the game when the coach wants, he's out of here. If he can't conform to the rules and regulations, he's out of here. That's what happened with the Lakers. Maybe that's why Phil Jackson won a world championship and why I probably wouldn't have.

Jackson said, "I'm not going to let Dennis Rodman bring down all of Chicago, bring down the entire team. We're going to use Dennis Rodman. We're going to get what we can out of him, march on and win the world title."

That's what they did. Would I have done that? Probably not, and I probably would have gotten fired. Jackson? He got mega, mega dollars, signing with the Lakers for $24 million over four years. It will be interesting to follow Rodman for a five-, six-year period when he's away from the spotlight. I'll be really curious to see what he does, what he turns into.

My theory has always been that once an athlete gets out of the limelight and has to find a real job in which to make a living, they don't get those second and third chances anymore. Because when you go into the work force and you have a problem, you know what happens? Nobody cares. No one is going to say, "We're going to help you get eligible for our corporate team." They could care less. They make you walk, baby. The party's over.

That's what happens to a lot of those guys who never learned how to treat people with respect. I believe we all make mistakes in life, but when a kid starts getting involved with drugs and alcohol, it's tough. One way to beat that thing is to not start. You start and every day is a war.

The NBA has always taken a hard line on major drugs like cocaine. Three strikes and you're out of the league. Three chances are enough to prove whether you've made good decisions and have the ability to be part of the NBA. At least it sends a message to the players that the league isn't going to tolerate the drug scene, yet if they do make a mistake, they're provided with an opportunity for rehabilitation. They're not just cast aside, which shows some compassion, some heart.

But again, in the corporate world, do you have that many opportunities? Three times? If you have a problem that deep, I don't think you should be in a uniform. You should be more concerned with getting your life in order.

The NBA, concerned about the rise in use of marijuana among its players and the fact that Chris Webber, Mookie Blaylock, Vernon Maxwell and J.R. Rider have been arrested on marijuana-related charges in the past, has put out a new policy. Players who test positive at training camp must undergo a mandatory counseling program. A second positive test is a $15,000 fine, and a third results in a five-game suspension. After that, you're gone.

Steroids were added to the league's banned substance list, although Androstenedione, the testosterone-producing substance formerly taken by Mark McGwire, is not on the list. Colleges have random drug testing. If you make a mistake like that, you've got to pay for that mistake. It should be a privilege to wear that uniform. We make it easy for people to get back into that uniform and we shouldn't.

So how do we control this problem that's forcing coaches into poor decisions, bringing ill-prepared kids into school and ultimately opening the door to violence, drugs and other problems? First, I think we should make it harder to get into that uniform in the first place. And I'm glad to see some programs agree with me. More and more schools are taking a

harder line in recruiting, taking a more careful look at the 17-
, 18-, 19-year-old kids they're bringing to campus.

Virginia Tech, which had 19 athletes arrested 22 times
in 13 months in 1995-96, said recruiters should be expected
to interview the person who, aside from the high school
coaches, is in the best position to know the recruit's personal background. That includes asking a list of questions about
fighting, alcohol or drug abuse, class attendance, violations of
the law, respect for authority, respect for others and social
skills.

All state colleges in Idaho, including Boise State, Idaho
and Idaho State, must abide by a three-year-old state board
of education policy prohibiting the recruitment of a player
convicted of a felony or any juvenile charge corresponding to
a felony. That decision came in response to 12 Boise State
football players being arrested in three years.

"I believe universities should not offer a scholarship to
someone convicted of a felony crime," said Jeff Benedict,
author and former director of the Center for Study of Sport in
Society. "Schools should not reward athletes who commit
crimes."

With that in mind, coaches need more of an opportunity to get to know the kid they're recruiting. Right now, the
three-week summer observation period restricts a coach from
really getting to know a kid as a person, getting to know his
family. College coaches have the responsibility of evaluating
and making sure they come up with kids who stick to a code
of conduct they'd like in their program. But once a recruit
gets to campus, you can do only so much.

Years ago, when I was coaching, you had an unlimited
number of times where you could go out and get to know a
kid and his family. Today you're allowed only five contacts. It
makes it a lot more difficult for a coach. What happens now
is you go to the high school and ask, "Hey, coach, tell me
about Johnny Jones." The stock answer, "He's the greatest
kid in the world." And you find out later the kid has a back-

ground like a rap sheet. How much honesty is there? Nobody tells you the truth, basically, when you come to visit. Certain schools like Duke benefit because of their power and stature. They can immediately lock up a kid who combines great grades and athletic ability. But others don't have that option.

Coaches want to win, and if they don't win, they know that, bang, they're gone, baby. So they take that chance. The media scrutiny and TV exposure have really increased the pressure to win. The dollars have gone up, the contracts have gone up for coaches. But the first time a kid slips, here come the newspaper columns calling for the coach's hide. Guys can say it doesn't bother them, but many of them are in tears.

Whenever I speak to youngsters I tell them that life isn't easy. It has its ups and downs. One day you might have to deal with the loss of an eye, like I did. Or maybe it'll be a broken marriage or an unfortunate accident. But you can't run every time problems occur. You have to be prepared to handle the good times with the bad. That's the real test.

Campus Chaos

I still can't understand why the NCAA didn't give Temple guard Rasheed Brokenborough an extra year of eligibility after this former Prop. 48 graduated in four years. Photo 6-1. facing page (courtesy of Temple University)

Chapter

6

Student-Athletes First

*The college entrance examination shouldn't be the sole
determinant for student-athlete admission*

There are nearly one million high school football players
and about 500,000 high school basketball players in the
United States. Of those, roughly 150 will make it to the NFL
and 50 to an NBA team. The odds of a high school football

player making it to the pros at all, let alone having a career, are about 6,000 to 1. The odds for a high school basketball player: 10,000 to 1. Less than 3 percent of college seniors will play even one year of professional basketball.

With those odds, kids need to get into the game as quickly as possible. It's also a big reason why freshman eligibility remains a difficult rule to reverse. Freshmen have been eligible to play varsity basketball since 1972. Perhaps the most heralded splash came in 1992 when Michigan's Fab Five — a freshman starting five of Chris Webber, Ray Jackson, Jalen Rose, Jimmy King and Juwan Howard — reached the NCAA championship game.

It was a different world from the days of old when guys like Lew Alcindor, Jerry West and Bill Bradley had to play on the freshman team before moving on to the varsity. The argument then, which is gaining popularity now, is that the year away from the bright lights allowed kids to become comfortable with their new surroundings and the pressures of college life.

I, for one, think that strategy was on target. Today's kids are too rushed, which is one of the major contributors to terrible graduation rates and early defections or transfers. I'm not alone in this thinking, of course. Jim Delany, the Big Ten commissioner, has been a vocal critic of the excesses of today's athletic climate. In 1998, Delany, a former player at North Carolina and investigator with the NCAA, sent a letter to the NCAA council of presidents and chancellors outlining a reform package he thinks is overdue because the college game is veering way off the path. If he had his way, he would:

- make freshmen ineligible for men's basketball but allow four years of eligibility.

- require that junior college kids transferring to four-year schools sit out two years.

Richard Hamilton became the star of stars in St. Petersburg as Connecticut, which defeated Ohio State in the NCAA semifinals at Tropicana Field, won its first national title two nights later with a win over Duke. Photo 6-2. (AP Photo).

- increase scholarships for men's basketball from 13 to 15, but allow no more than four in a year and no more than seven over two years.

- eliminate summer recruiting, with all evaluations to occur during the school year, which would rid the game of what he calls an "elite subculture" that spawns middlemen.

- encourage shoe and apparel manufacturers to withdraw from promotion and sponsorship of non-school-based camps and competition.

He takes his points further. In his mind, the success of the NCAA Tournament has obscured some fundamental problems. Specifically, it has spawned:

- a decline in graduation rates. According to the latest NCAA statistics, only 41 percent of male basketball players in the 1991 entering class got their degrees, including just 37 percent of black players. That compares with 50 percent for football and 66 percent for women's basketball players. The graduation rate for all Division I athletes was 57 percent.

- an increase in the number of players leaving programs, either for the pros or more playing time at other schools. In the Big Ten from 1990 to 1997, Delany says, 101 of 193 recruited athletes left, with 70 percent transferring.

Delany says he is not näive, that he knows this is an uphill battle. He knows getting rid of the summer observation period would meet with opposition. After all, the NCAA implemented the summer period restrictions in the early 1980's as a cost-cutting measure, and many small schools thrive on reduced costs. Getting shoe companies out of the picture won't be easy either.

Making freshmen ineligible for men's basketball scares some people only because of the possibility of legal action, in Delany's opinion. The Big Ten's idea is to allow freshmen to practice with the varsity after January 1 and play a ten-game schedule, most of which would be played on weekends and involve only local travel.

A blue-ribbon panel of 27 Division I coaches and administrators convened to evaluate methods to reform college basketball. The panel, chaired by Syracuse University chancellor Kenneth Shaw, has studied a number of proposals, including the idea of making male freshman players ineligible. The study was prompted by concerns over poor graduation rates, a freshman's ability to adapt to college life, and the greater willingness of underclassmen to jump to the NBA.

According to Kentucky athletic director C.M. Newton, all three ex-coaches on the Division I Working Group to Study Basketball Issues, himself, former North Carolina coach Dean Smith and Virginia AD Terry Holland, lobbied for freshman ineligibility. But when the panel issued its report in July 1999, it stopped short of recommending freshman ineligibility to the NCAA board of directors because it lacked sufficient support.

It was successful in advancing the concern about graduation rates. It tied scholarships to academic performances, rewarding schools that graduate players and penalizing those that don't. Under "The Graduation/Good Standing Rate," schools that graduate players at a rate of 75 percent or higher, excluding transfers and those who leave for the pros in good academic standing, would receive an additional 14th scholarship. Schools in the 33-74 percent range would remain at 13 scholarships. And schools with rates of 32 percent or less could award only 12 grants in aid. Rates would be computed across four incoming classes, with each class being given a six-year window to graduate.

"The idea is basically a scheme of rewards and punishments,' Shaw said. 'We got tired of hearing schools say, 'Well, a lot of them went pro or transferred.'"

The members of the panel should be saluted. They're trying to do what they think is best for the game. I like how the panel wants to compute graduation rates. It proposes that schools not be penalized for transfers or players who leave early for the pros as long as they're in good standing academically. The way it's currently done is a joke.

That said, one problem I see is that I don't buy the idea that a coach will be motivated enough to earn one extra scholarship. First of all, many schools can survive on 12 scholarship players. That's one less hassle for a coach to deal with and more PT for everybody else.

What it does more than anything is create positive publicity for schools that do graduate more than 75 percent, and it becomes an embarrassment for those who graduate less than 32 percent. The numbers would be right out there for you to look at. Another measure proposed by the group is to place a limit on the number of scholarships offered each year. The panel suggested a maximum of four, an idea designed to prevent coaches from running players off and restocking their rosters every year.

The panel made three other recommendations to improve academics:

- Encourage, but don't require, basketball players to attend summer school prior to their first fall semester. Schools could provide financial aid for any student who takes a minimum of six hours of summer courses.

- Permit financial aid to academic non-qualifiers.

- Require academic qualifiers to complete a minimum of 12 hours toward a degree with a 2.0 GPA after their first semester of their freshman year.

The idea of summer school is fantastic. The NCAA should require incoming freshmen to take six credit hours, especially in cases in which high school has been an unbelievable challenge for a player and he's really had to squeeze by to make the necessary numbers to be eligible. You're not hurting the youngster; you're helping him, making the transition from high school to college easier.

If the NCAA member schools pass these proposals, they could go into effect for the 2000-01 season. But it's clear freshman ineligibility may not become a reality. The concerns over the legality of such legislation are too strong. Still, if the bottom line is to improve graduation rates, there is no doubt in my mind that freshmen should be ineligible. Just recently, some high school kids were quoted as saying, "Hey, if there's freshmen ineligibility, a lot of the top ten seniors will go pro." So be it. Let them go to the NBA.

The college game will still reign supreme because of the spirit and enthusiasm. Whenever the TV listings read North Carolina-Duke, Michigan-Indiana, UCLA-Arizona, there will still be excitement galore. Hey, we're still going to have my Diaper Dandies and my All-Rolls-Roycers, baby.

Will kids who leave early or avoid college altogether be missed? Of course. But as long as the college game is being used as a short-term springboard for one-year wonders, not only will the college game suffer, but also, increasingly, the biggest loser of all will be the NBA. Why? Because most of these kids aren't ready for the league. And sadly, many times the losers are the kids themselves.

Delany conceded that making freshmen ineligible could encourage some to go straight from high school to the NBA. "But those players won't be in school very long anyway," he says.

What started with a proposal to improve the quality of academics in men's basketball has since developed into a raging debate. *USA Today* supported Delany's views on freshman ineligibility in an editorial, claiming the NCAA had its heart in

133

the right place when it put college-bound students on notice that academics take priority over sports, but that, in practice, testing standards have done little to ensure that male basketball players leave with college degrees.

In a second editorial, after the paper got word that the panel would not recommend freshman ineligibility, *USA Today* wrote: "The coaches and athletic directors who once dominated NCAA policy-making while college presidents looked the other way are whining about extra costs and difficulties recruiting high school hotshots."

The low graduation rates have been blamed by some on the high proportion of African-American players, many from poor families and low-budget public school systems, that basketball draws. Only 37 percent of African-American male basketball players from the 1991 survey graduated. But only 45 percent of the white players did. Freshman ineligibility, *USA Today* argued, would allow those players to adjust to academics before they have to deal with basketball's tough two-semester schedule.

I couldn't have said it better myself. And I've pushed for freshman ineligibility many times. In fact, I think if we want to solve the academic problems and have the graduation rate grow from an all-time low for basketball players, that's the way to go. If you want to create the idea of the student-athlete, instead of an athlete-student, freshman ineligibility would be a positive.

Freshman ineligibility would give a youngster a chance to get acclimated to college because he'd get a chance to adjust to pressure. People have no clue about the pressure. Think about normal students. When they go to college, they experience the tension, the anxiety and the fears. They're going to meet a new roommate for the first time. They don't know where the buildings are. They have no clue where their classes are. There's a lot of anxiety.

Well, combine that with playing football or basketball and the pressure to excel and perform in that arena in front of 15,000 screaming maniacs, me included. It's really a tense time, especially for kids who come in as academic risks.

I'd rather see kids sit out that first year and play on the freshman team. I don't see anything wrong with that. Now, there will be some kids, one-year wonders or two-year wonders, who might decide to jump immediately to the NBA because they don't want to be part of a situation like that.

Well, you know what I say to that? That kid never wanted to go to college anyway. Let him move on. In football, it should be no problem because most players red-shirt anyway and spend a year in the weight room to build themselves up physically. In basketball, a lot of schools use freshman eligibility as a recruiting tool, telling kids they can come in and play right away and be a major factor, that they can help that team grow.

With freshman ineligibility, the rich would get richer. Think about it. Right now a school like Gonzaga can attract a player who can be an instant star as a Diaper Dandy because at most of the big schools, young stars need to wait for PT to free up. That extra incentive to go to a small school would be somewhat erased if freshmen were ineligible. Limited recruiting periods help the marquee programs. Because of their reputations, they don't need as much time to sell a kid. What a smaller school has to do is hope there are some late-blooming kids out there, kids who are overlooked by the big schools and who are available to them, like a David Robinson who went to Navy.

Some coaches agree with me, some don't. No surprise there. North Carolina basketball coach Bill Guthridge, whose school has long been in favor of freshman ineligibility, would take the plan a step further, making freshmen ineligible in all sports.

"That would send a powerful message that academics come first," he says.

I buy that. I think all sports should fall into that category because all those kids face those kinds of pressures. I'd like to see freshmen ineligible but have four years of varsity eligibility. Five years to play four. I also don't think you should have a full freshmen season. Start in January, after completing the first semester, and play weekend games against local schools, junior colleges, so there's no overnight travel involved.

Penn State basketball coach Jerry Dunn thinks the extra first year would ease the pressure of school and sports that athletes face and give them more time to mature. But former Georgetown coach John Thompson says it's unreasonable to tell an athlete he can't have anything to do with his sport for 12 months.

Lute Olson of Arizona feels there are too many reasons why a rule like this would never pass. If they were to do that, he says, they would have to increase the current scholarships from 13 to 18, or at least to 16, so teams would have a period to adjust and have enough players in the program. He is against having players begin play after the first semester, saying it would be impossible to build team chemistry. He also feels new players would fall too far behind from lack of practice.

I don't buy all of Delany's proposals. For instance, his plan that calls for junior college and foreign players to sit out one year and for transfers to sit out two has holes. The American Civil Liberties Union would jump all over that one, and junior college presidents would go ballistic. If a kid goes to junior college and has earned his degree so he can eventually play major college basketball, he should not have to give up a third year. I don't think that's fair.

Jim Haney, the executive director of the National Association of Basketball Coaches and a member of the committee, says, "The real problem is that too many players are majoring in eligibility, taking the minimum number of the

Big Ten commissioner Jim Delany (right) is an advocate of strong NCAA regulation of recruiting and academic standards for student- athletes. Here he is with Michigan State coach Tom Izzo following the Big Ten Tournament victory. Photo 6-3. (courtesy of MSU Sports)

easiest possible classes to remain full-time students and achieve acceptable grade point averages."

Many parents and prospective college athletes already object to the idea of freshman ineligibility. The *Des Moines Register* interviewed Iowa's best high school prospect, 6-8 forward Glen Worley of Iowa City West, and Bob Horner, the father and coach of a super prospect, sophomore guard Jeff Horner from Mason City, and got negative feedback on the idea.

"Sure, there are going to be some players who can't handle the change in college life," Worley told the *Register*, "but that doesn't mean all of us can't." Worley committed to Iowa well before leaving high school. Horner committed to Iowa after his freshman season.

At the root of the freshman ineligibility issue is the NCAA's desire to improve its poor graduation rates. The *St. Petersburg Times* ran a huge story on academics and grad rates during the 1999 Final Four held in that city. The moral of its story: No matter what colleges do to push players toward graduation, the results are discouraging.

A review of the Final Four teams tells me all I need to know. Of the freshmen entering during the school years of 1989-90 through 1992-93, Duke graduated 82 percent of its players, Michigan State graduated 73 percent, UConn 47 percent and Ohio State 21 percent. Of course, these numbers count early departures and transfers as "non-graduates," which as I said earlier is a joke. Still, these are startling statistics, but schools are trying.

UConn flew tutors in to help players on road trips. Michigan State recently built a massive 31,000 square-foot academic center. Ohio State has mandatory study halls, counselors and academic mentors to teach players life skills. When the school gave AD Andy Geiger a new five-year deal that pays him $250,000 a year, it included incentives for the percentage of student-athletes with grade point averages of at least 3.0 and graduation rates of those athletes.

The University of California at Berkeley has instituted a six-week Summer Bridge program designed to give new Cal students intensive college preparation prior to their fall semester. It's intended to help freshmen get acclimated to both the academic and social sides of campus life. And it's not easy. The student-athlete participants, including recruits in basketball and football, are scheduled from 8 a.m. to 10 p.m.

One sticking point to the freshman ineligibility issue is the number of scholarships available to each school. Schools now have just 13 scholarships to give for men's college basketball, down from the 15 they used to have. The NCAA reduced the number to 14 in August 1992, then to 13 in August 1993.

My gut feeling is that the reduction of scholarships didn't affect programs as much as many thought it might. But once you start talking about fielding freshman teams, you have to think about increasing the number of scholarships again, probably back to 15.

But here's the bad news in that scenario. In all likelihood, the major powers simply could grab two more blue-chippers. It would also be contradictory to what most schools are doing to comply with Title IX. But there are a number of proposals being floated out there beyond Delany and the Big Ten. The SEC is backing an idea introduced by Vanderbilt AD Todd Turner, who proposes that a university could no longer reassign the scholarship of an athlete who flunks out until after his class graduates. The SEC presidents like it, but it hasn't received much support around the league.

I've said that myself. You reward schools if they graduate players. I think five years is plenty of time for a kid to graduate. If schools stay on top of their players and guide them, the players should be able to graduate in that time frame. It would force schools to recruit a better level of kid, a legitimate student-athlete, to avoid losing scholarships. Of course, we have to factor in kids who leave early for the pros.

Do the schools get special exemptions? My feeling is that if a kid leaves early, the school shouldn't be penalized.

I think one major factor contributing to the need for freshman ineligibility is the over-saturation of summer camps and tournaments. Many of the better high school players have become vagabonds, flying all over the country during the three-week observation period in July with their club teams. They show up at both the Nike and Adidas super camps, then go on to places like Las Vegas, Augusta, Orlando, Long Beach and San Diego to play in huge all-star tournaments.

The NCAA's Cedric Dempsey is upset over what he calls the "summer exploitation going on with high profile basketball players", their exposure to agents and other bad influences. "What they bring to campus in the first year is an expectation of how they've been treated throughout the summer," he says.

A lot of fingers are being pointed at the Nike and Adidas camps, which attract 90 percent of the best prospects in early July. Shoe company camps have become the primary sources of evaluation for coaches. Some coaches and administrators are pushing for reform to summer recruiting. Among other things, they want to:

- chop the current three-and-a-half-week July observation period for college coaches to seven days. The remaining evaluation days would be reallocated to the winter months when prospects are playing for their high school teams. Ideally, this gets the high school coach back as the focal point of the recruiting process.

- allow college coaches to telephone recruits once a week starting on June 1 prior to their senior seasons. Currently, coaches are not allowed contact with a recruit until July 1. This would allow colleges to better judge the interest a potential recruit has in their program before evaluating him in July.

- disallow or severely limit communications between college coaches and traveling team coaches during the spring and summer to keep the traveling team coach out of the process.

- establish regional development camps run by USA Basketball, which would provide a more structured environment for player evaluation and competition and limit the influence of shoe manufacturers during the summer.

Objections are certain to come from coaches of smaller schools, who believe they would be placed at a major disadvantage. Seeing hundreds of kids at one campus is a huge cost-cutting measure for programs with a limited budget. The hurdle, of course, is money. Both Nike and Adidas have it. The NCAA might not be interested in coughing up hundreds or thousands of dollars to make these changes. Officials at Nike and Adidas say they will run camps and AAU tournaments regardless of whether college coaches attend.

I don't like what's going on in the summer period either. The NCAA has got to jump in and change some of the rules, including giving the power back to the high school coaches and stripping it away from the coaches of the summer traveling teams. Kids are going from an environment where they play all summer, travel first class all over the country, and get the best uniforms and equipment with a summer all-star team, then turn around and have to play for their less-flashy high school teams.

Getting those coaches out of the recruiting game is a must. I don't want to indict all of these folks because there are some really good people out there in AAU who have good motives. But there are more who don't, and that's sad. Hey, there's nothing wrong with kids competing against the best and learning where they fit in as long as there are some rules. The panel considered either deregulating or abolishing summer recruiting altogether but decided to recommend some changes instead. Specifically:

- Shift blocks of time in which college coaches can evaluate and contact recruits from the summer to the academic year.

- Limit evaluations during the academic year to regularly scheduled events and eliminate all tournaments during the academic year not run directly by high schools or junior colleges. That would eliminate many AAU and traveling team tournaments.

- Adopt an extensive certification process of summer events.

The certification process is designed to keep outside parties — shoe companies, agents, etc. — from tainting the summer recruiting process. A vital part of the certification process is requiring financial disclosure of the funding for summer travel teams.

"We're asking for full financial disclosure as a way of getting after this," Newton says. There would also be an NCAA "watchdog committee" formed to monitor basketball recruiting practices.

If I had my way, I'd also limit the observation period to two weeks in the summer and allow college coaches to evaluate prospects throughout the high school season. I don't buy that high school kids being recruited during the season presents a problem. I don't buy that it'll affect them academically. Come on. All that is nonsense. If Bob Knight had his way, the summer observation period would be completely wiped out and players would be evaluated with only a high school coach or assistant present. He's at least getting people to talk about alternatives.

I remember when I was an assistant at Rutgers, one of the prized recruits I targeted was the high school player of the year, Phil Sellers of Thomas Jefferson High in Brooklyn.

Sellers was being courted by everyone. My buddy from TV land, Digger Phelps, actually led the recruiting wars for him when he was coaching at Notre Dame, and ultimately received a commitment.

But Sellers later reneged and joined us at Rutgers where he eventually helped take Rutgers to the Final Four in 1976. Let me tell you, during that period of time my wife thought I had a girlfriend on the side, because every night my evening ended with a phone call to Phil, and every morning started with a drive over to Brooklyn to say hi to his coach, guidance counselor and Phil himself. Man, did I love to recruit when I was an assistant at Rutgers and later a head coach at Detroit. There were no NCAA restrictions then, so we did it every day, all year round, until the March signing date.

Times have changed. Let me tell you, there's no chance in the world for a little school, which Rutgers was at the time, to land a player like Sellers with today's rules. Today, most kids sign in the early period in the second week of November. I have no problem with that as long as a kid has qualified academically. But it's absurd when so many kids who aren't even close to making their grades commit early.

Alumni get all fired up, they have a blue-chip recruiting class, and then find out in April and May that three or four of the kids who signed never projected. It's embarrassing for the kids, the coaching staff and the university. A lot of great recruiting classes in November fizzle by the spring. Sometimes a school will lock up a kid based on what he's done as a high school junior and then realize he's not that good. The kid gets a little cocky and doesn't perform like he did up to that point.

One more thing that really bugs me about recruiting is players who sign early and commit to a school early should have the right to be re-recruited if the coach at that school leaves for another job. I don't want to hear the argument that the kid is supposed to make a decision on the university, not the coach. That is Dark Ages thinking. Ninety percent of the kids are deciding on a college because they want to play for a particular coach and believe they'll fit into his system.

Sean Connolly, a shooting guard from Massachusetts, signed with Providence a couple of years ago because he was under the assumption that Pete Gillen was to be the coach and he would be playing for him. Then Gillen went to Virginia. Now the kid had to stay there or miss a year if he transferred without the school's consent. That's absurd. Why is the kid an afterthought in this situation? The coach leaves, lands a huge contract with a country club membership, and the recruits get to wait to see for whom they'll be playing. Even those coaches would tell you a kid should be allowed to be re-recruited.

Here's my plan; give the new coach two weeks to convince a kid to stay. After that, he should be fair game...pure, simple and fair.

As for Connolly, he started as a freshman for Providence, didn't like it, and then decided to transfer to Ohio State at the end of his first year. We saw what happened at Kentucky after Tubby Smith took over for Rick Pitino. Myron Anthony, Michael Bradley and Ryan Hogan all signed there two years ago. All of them left. Why? Michael Bradley's father will tell you his son signed to play for Pitino. He went there and played for Tubby but never felt comfortable. I think a recruit should have a two-week period to change his mind if the coach leaves, but the player has not yet enrolled.

I like what some of the great prospects are doing now. They want to protect themselves against coaches leaving, so they verbally commit or sign a scholarship form with the school instead of a national letter of intent. Jason Kapono, a McDonald's All-America forward from Artesia, Calif., did just that with UCLA. It doesn't work for mid-major prospects that don't have the leverage to keep a school on hold until spring to see if the coach is still there. The school may award that scholarship to someone else. But it's not a bad idea if you can get away with it.

One other way a kid can avoid the letter-of-intent route. Study hard and go to one of the Ivy League schools, which don't award athletic scholarships, so they're not part of the national letter of intent. See, studying hard has its advantages.

It seems that so many of these kids want playing time immediately because they're chasing that pro dream, and I think that's why we're seeing so many transfers. After the 1999 season alone, guys like Kentucky's Bradley, Ryan Humphrey of Oklahoma, Adam Harrington of North Carolina State and Maurice Evans of Wichita State left for greener pastures. I hope it works out for them, but some kids just don't understand that when you run from problems or from situations that aren't exactly what you envisioned, you could end up running the rest of your life.

Now, in some cases, transferring is justified. I really believe if a coach is willing to let go of a player who's doing nothing but grabbing pine, that player shouldn't have to sit out the year. But a kid who's a vital part of the program, that's another thing.

If all these problems weren't enough, we can't overlook one of the most obvious areas of concern: meddling boosters. These are the zealots who want to be the Mr. Big on campus and will do anything to prove it. In many cases, their meddling simply starts with the love of their university and a simple desire to help. But when they do things that interfere with the program, that's when major problems occur.

I think the NCAA took a giant step in 1991 when it prohibited alumni from calling or writing to prospective student-athletes. In 99.9 percent of the cases, the coaches themselves are not going to cheat. There's too much at stake, especially among the elite programs, because the financial stakes are too great. To risk all that, an individual has to be wacky.

But there are always exceptions. After investigators discovered that Lester Earl, a McDonald's All-America forward from Baton Rouge, La., received a $5,000 cash payment from a booster in 1996 while the school was recruiting him, the NCAA drilled LSU with probation for the 1998-99 season, lowered scholarships from 13 to 11 and limited the school to four new scholarships through 2000. Earl, who eventually transferred to Kansas after the first semester of his freshman year, actually walked away from the wreckage unscathed by testifying against his old school.

He had a fourth year of eligibility restored by the Collegiate Commissioners Association when he appealed his original letter of intent with LSU, which required him to fulfill one full year of residency at LSU or forfeit a year of eligibility. Earl's decision to spill his guts to the NCAA really burned former LSU coach Dale Brown. Brown, who had out-recruited Kansas for Earl, was furious and was on the phone with a Kansas City radio station the day the probation hit. He blasted the people at Kansas for getting involved with Earl.

Let's be real; the bottom line is if Kansas and Roy Williams didn't pursue Earl when he made himself available to them, 50 other schools would have lined up in Baton Rouge to get their hands on a 6-9 rebounding machine. Williams was able to come out with the recruiting victory when Earl decided to transfer because of their prior relationship. Kansas AD Bob Frederick said Brown's claims were ludicrous. Check the phone records, he said.

My feelings are that if Roy Williams had to do it again, he probably never would have taken the kid and gone through the unbelievable nightmare it caused. Based on the facts, Earl was not innocent. I feel that he should have been declared ineligible, by the NCAA, for violating NCAA rules. If Earl really felt bad about it, he should have made his complaint known to the NCAA when he was being recruited in an illegal fashion. He should have stood up tall and talked about it. Instead, allegedly he took what he could.

I have a problem with that. Most coaches I've talked to have a problem with the fact that a player like Earl could testify against his old school then receive eligibility at a new school. Why should he be rewarded while his former school suffers when he was one of the guilty parties in the first place? That Earl testified against LSU and got immunity from the NCAA doesn't sit well with me.

My feeling is that if a player has admitted he received illegal inducements to go to a given school, he should now be banned from playing college ball. Why should he be rewarded while his former school is penalized? That's what bothers me about a lot of the penalties that are incurred.

At LSU, the new coach, John Brady, comes in, steps onto the sideline and has to pay for all the problems that occurred during the previous regime. That's not fair. Rather than penalizing the innocent, punish the ones who are responsible for the actions that took place.

But I guess when you think about it, what else can the NCAA do? What penalty can it pass on other than to penalize the school? In some cases, the NCAA has been more lenient when the offending school makes a coaching change. After looking into recruiting violations in Alabama's basketball program, the NCAA exonerated the school but hit a former assistant coach hard. Tyrone Beaman was suspended after he was accused of asking two boosters, Montgomery lawyers Charles Stakely and Truman Hobbs Jr., for $5,000 to create a slush fund for two blue-chip prospects from Texas in 1997.

But the boosters reported the request to the university, which in turn notified the NCAA. The NCAA said in February 1999 that if any school wishes to hire Beaman in the next four years, it must get clearance from the infractions committee. It praised Alabama for its handling of the case.

Rick Neuheisel, the new Washington football coach, allegedly had five assistants visit five blue-chip prospects the Sunday before signing day, which is technically a dead, or quiet, period in which all contacts are barred. The school found out about it and self-reported to the NCAA. The school declared all five of the athletes, who did indeed sign with

Washington, ineligible. Washington then petitioned the NCAA, which restored their eligibility.

The five coaches each were withheld from two weeks of off-campus recruiting in May and two weeks in the December-January contact period. The Pac-10 voted to accept Washington's self-imposed penalties, which included limiting Neuheisel to nine evaluation days, rather than the normal 29, during the 1999-2000 spring and fall periods. The school will be allowed six fewer official visits next year. No football players currently enrolled at Colorado will be permitted to transfer to Washington and compete for the Huskies.

NCAA investigators looked into allegations that a DePaul player had bought a video game for then-recruit Quentin Richardson with money provided by a DePaul assistant coach. The school conducted its own investigation and found that a player took a prospective recruit to a strip club. But James P. Doyle, the school's vice president for student affairs, said the visit was not condoned by the coaching staff and therefore did not violate NCAA rules.

The only infraction investigators found? Two recruits were served pizza in DePaul's locker room after a game. The two players involved with serving the pizza have since donated the cost to charity. I wonder if it was plain or came with everything on it?

One way the NCAA has attempted to help improve its academic standards was its implementation in 1994 of the NCAA Clearinghouse. The idea was an attempt to make sure that all scholarship players met similar academic standards for entry into college. Sounds like a good idea, right? It was, but it has become a nightmare.

The Clearinghouse creates more problems than it solves because the information takes too long to gather. There has to be a better way to decide what's a legitimate class and what isn't. If anything, that should be left to the discretion of each school. If a school says a class is part of its curriculum, who is the Clearinghouse to say that the credits shouldn't be accepted?

Some kids decide to take matters into their own hands. Center Kenny Thomas of New Mexico started his college career with a lawsuit against the NCAA and received an injunction so he could play as a freshman. Apparently when he was in ninth grade, he took a science course on the advice of a counselor. Later, the NCAA claimed the course did not meet the core curriculum requirement. After his sophomore year of college, Thomas and the NCAA reached an agreement. He would sit out the first semester of his senior year.

To me, this is flat-out wrong. It wasn't Thomas' fault. The kid took the course thinking it was OK, then found out later it was a course that the NCAA wouldn't approve. There is a happy ending, though. Thomas stayed all four years and was a first-round pick in the 1999 draft, going 22nd to the Houston Rockets.

Aside from checking the student's transcripts to make sure he meets certain criteria, the NCAA has also had to get into the business of confirming whether a prospect's standardized test scores are valid. The case of onetime Southern California hotshot Schea Cotton demonstrates just how tough that feat can be. After he led Mater Dei High to the state title as a sophomore in 1995, *Sports Illustrated* ran a story in which Cotton was talking about turning pro once he graduated high school. That fairy tale never came true.

Cotton ripped up his shoulder and missed all but 11 games the next two years. He originally signed with Long Beach State to play with his brother, James, but got a release after James turned pro a year early. Then he was headed for UCLA but was declared ineligible in September when the NCAA invalidated his original SAT score, claiming the exam was printed in large type and he was given extra time to work on it even though he didn't have a learning disability.

So Cotton enrolled at St. Thomas More, a prep school in Connecticut, then signed a letter of intent with North

Carolina State. But the NCAA still said he was ineligible. Cotton eventually surfaced at Long Beach City College, where he became a star. Cotton's family sued the NCAA in September 1998, and the organization finally ruled him eligible in January 1999.

N.C. State tried to get back in with Cotton, but the kid's family was upset that the school hadn't hung in with him during the crisis. Cotton eventually wound up at Alabama, where he started the 1999-2000 season. Mark Gottfried, the head coach there, had recruited Cotton when he was an assistant at UCLA, and the family felt comfortable with the situation. At least the kid is persistent.

But why did it have to happen? Since the early 1980's, the NCAA has issued several decrees addressing student-athlete eligibility standards and graduation rates. The flurry of bureaucratic activity came in response to horror stories about athletes like Kevin Ross of Creighton, who had a college degree but couldn't read. The television magazine "*60 Minutes*" was all over that one.

The NCAA originally established eligibility standards in 1973, requiring that an athlete graduate high school with a 2.0 GPA. In 1983, a group of college presidents, sponsored by the American Council on Education, proposed minimum academic standards for freshman athletics eligibility. The result was Proposition 48, enacted in 1986.

That created a new standard, which required a minimum 700 score on the SAT or 15 on the ACT and a 2.0 grade point average in 11 core courses. Activists rebelled, but Proposition 48 did what its proponents said it would; it raised graduation rates. College presidents were so pleased, they increased the standards in 1992 to require a 2.5 GPA in 13 courses with the same SAT and ACT minimum score. This action was known as Proposition 42. Finally, a sliding scale was put into effect four years later, known as Proposition 16.

The NCAA used to severely penalize Proposition 48 recruits. First, the kid lost a year of eligibility. He also couldn't practice with the team, which I could never understand. Why wouldn't you want a kid to at least be around the team under the jurisdiction of a coach, who could supervise, organize and watch what that youngster is doing?

By leaving him out, you basically turned him over to the street. Now, at least, if you're a partial qualifier, i.e. one who has a 2.5 or better GPA but not a high-enough score on the ACT or the SAT, the NCAA will let you practice and, if you're on target to get a degree, grant a fifth year of eligibility.

According to the NCAA Guide to the College Bound Student-Athlete, before qualifying for a Division I college, you must:

- graduate high school.

- successfully complete a core curriculum of at least 13 academic courses (including at least four years of English, two of math, two in the social sciences, two in natural or physical science, one additional course in English, math or natural or physical science, and two additional academic courses from either a foreign language, computer science, philosophy or non-doctrinal religion).

- have a grade point average and a combined score on the SAT verbal and math sections or a sum score on the ACT based on the qualifier index scale shown in the following table.

Core GPA	ACT	SAT
2.500	68	820
2.475	69	830
2.450	70	840-850
2.425	70	860
2.400	71	860
2.375	72	870
2.350	74	880
2.325	75	900
2.275	76	910
2.250	77	920
2.225	78	930
2.200	79	940
2.175	80	950
2.150	80	960
2.125	81	960
2.100	82	970
2.075	83	980
2.050	84	990
2.025	85	1000
2.000	86	1010

Wow. I'm glad I'm not trying to qualify now, man. But all that could change. In March 1999, U.S. District Court Judge Ronald L. Buckwalter ruled that test score requirements violated federal civil rights law because of their "unjustified" impact on African-Americans. Buckwalter cited NCAA data showing that an average of 19.8 percent of the African-American male athletes that Division I schools were interested in recruiting failed to meet the minimum over the last five years. The figure for white men was 4.2 percent.

Buckwalter ruled that minimum standardized test scores were unfair. The ruling came as a result of a lawsuit filed by four African-American athletes who claimed they were denied scholarships or eligibility because they did not meet the minimum test score.

The National Association of Basketball Coaches has always been against the SAT being the determinant that makes a prospect eligible. Oklahoma basketball coach Kelvin Sampson wants to keep the eligibility requirement of 13 core courses with a minimal 2.5 grade point average, but eliminate the SAT or ACT score from the equation. Some say scores should be part of a formula as long as there isn't an absolute cut-off based on test scores.

Others, like Temple University basketball coach John Chaney, suggest that the SAT and ACT be part of a review that includes teacher and guidance counselor recommendations and writing samples. "Countless young African-American men have been damaged since 1986," Chaney wrote in a *New York Times* Op-Ed, just after Judge Buckwalter's decision. "Let's give the new generation a chance, even if it means a chance to fail. Every college should be allowed to formulate its own admission plan and judge each student on a case-by-case basis. The time for mandating standardized test scores must end. It's already done enough harm."

Former Georgetown coach John Thompson agrees. "The tests were never intended to be used as a means to determine athletic eligibility," Thompson said. "It's not being used correctly. The NCAA ignored that. The tests are biased. The NCAA's own data said so. We beat them with their own stick."

Not everyone is in their corner. Many feel that minimum test standards are necessary. "Instituting standards doesn't mean we ignore the problems of the underclass, quite the contrary," says Penn State football coach Joe Paterno. "You have to address the problem of kids being raised by single parents or by no parents, but you don't help them by lowering the standards. ... We at universities have to attack the problem from our end by demanding certain standards for our kids to be eligible to play. That's the only way we'll keep pressure on athletically talented youngsters to realize their education comes first."

Columnist Bob Smizek of the *Pittsburgh Post Gazette* wrote, "African-Americans make up less than 15 percent of the population, but they represent 60 percent of the players starting in the Tournament. The fact is that for virtually every African-American that is denied eligibility, his place is taken by another African-American who is more qualified to do college work. This was not about denying opportunity, it was about allowing unprepared athletes to sit out their freshman season, away from the enormous time and energy demands of college sports, and get acclimated to college life."

High school officials have complained that the NCAA has usurped the role of school boards and education experts by failing to recognize the legitimacy of several acceptable high school courses. Civil rights groups have attacked the NCAA's use of standardized tests as biased against minorities, with 58 percent of the students denied freshman eligibility being African-American. If Buckwalter's ruling holds up against appeal, Proposition 16 athletes could become eligible immediately.

But the NCAA isn't going down without a fight. Its attorneys asked and received a stay, contending that without one, each institution would be free to adopt its own eligibility rules, which would thwart the NCAA's ultimate goal of creating an equal playing field. They got their wish on March 30, 1999, when the U.S. District Court of Appeals granted their motion until an appeal could be heard.

The decision temporarily reinstated Proposition 16 and allowed the NCAA board of directors to think about some alternatives. Among them:

- a single minimum grade point average in a specific number of courses.
- an extended sliding scale with a minimum grade point average.
- a full sliding scale.
- a combination of a sliding scale and grade point average above which a test score would not be considered.
- freshman ineligibility.

One reason why some people are intrigued with the idea of freshmen sitting out that first year is that men's basketball would no longer need instant eligibility standards. Schools could recruit whomever they wanted because that player would have a year to prove he could do the class work.

My feeling is that each school has its own mission, and that school's admissions department should have the right to determine whom it accepts and who qualifies at that school. There still should be core curriculum requirements because you have to have kids prepared in algebra, the sciences and languages to be able to sit in a classroom and compete at a basic level. I think admissions should be based more on what a kid has produced in his high school core curriculum classes. To me, that's more important than looking at the SAT's and ACT's. That would be a positive way to go and would eliminate the Proposition 48 or Proposition 42 tag these kids get stuck with. We're supposed to help kids, not hurt them.

Rasheed Brokenborough is proof enough to me that the system must change. Following the 1999 season, the Temple guard asked for and was denied an extra year of eligibility by the NCAA. Brokenborough was a non-qualifier when he entered college; he had neither the minimum GPA nor test score and had to borrow money and get conventional financial aid to fund his first year in school. He also had to sit out that year. He then went on to beat the odds, graduating in four years.

But the NCAA was unimpressed. "Our legislation does not permit a non-qualifier to get a fourth year of competition back," said Bob Oliver, an executive with the NCAA, "unless they fit into the category of a student with a diagnosed learning disability. That's our legislation."

Temple's John Chaney was incensed. "I think they're perfect snobs," he said. "They celebrate themselves, these people who sit in judgment of these kids, the presidents."

Ironically, if Brokenborough had been a partial qualifier or a learning-disabled non-qualifier, he would have had a shot at the waiver. A student who is learning disabled can complete 75 percent of graduation requirements and get the added year, while Brokenborough, who has completed 100 percent of those requirements, was shown the door. Bye-bye.

I really believe Brokenborough got a raw deal. I did a commentary about Rasheed and spoke to him, so I'm quite familiar with his situation. He graduated within the four-year period and should have been granted the extra year of eligibility. Here is a proud kid who does everything the right way, does everything in a legitimate fashion.

His grandmother said he's the first one in their family to graduate college and is so proud of him. His situation is another reason we talk about lunacy in rules, not using good common sense and good judgment. Here's an example of a lack of compassion and a lack of understanding. Sometimes you should throw rules out of the window, man, when you come down and see a kid like this.

Rasheed Brokenborough with his grandmother and coach Chaney at a Temple University awards ceremony. Photo 6-3. (courtesy Temple University).

Andre Miller of Utah was luckier. He came in as a Proposition 42 and had to sit out his freshman year. But he got the extra year because at least now the NCAA has taken the step of saying that if an athlete meets one of the two standards, either the GPA or the test score, he's a partial qualifier, and it will give him a chance to get the extra year back if he graduates on time. Andre did all that and then began working on his master's degree and wound up making first-team All-American.

If a kid is ineligible as a freshman and he's on target to graduate, he should be given a fourth year of eligibility. If he wants to graduate and move on, fine. But if he wants to stay that fifth year, let him play. I think Andre made the right choice. The Cleveland Cavaliers must have thought so too. They chose him with the eighth pick in the '99 NBA draft.

The other problem with relying on test scores is that there's always a temptation to change them. And it's not just kids doing it. The National Center for Fair and Open Testing claims that the number of reported instances of cheating by administrators, teachers and students is on the rise.

The Georgia Professional Standards Commission, for example, saw 25 cases of improper administration of tests from July 1998 to March 1999. The violations ranged from giving students answers to using practice tests based on the previous year's exams.

In Texas, criminal charges for altering students' records to improve school level test scores have been filed against one administrator, and the entire district faces civil charges and a fine. Investigations into erasures on test forms were ordered in Dallas and Houston, where a principal and three teachers have been asked to resign.

How much cheating is going on? I don't know, but I do know that kids are taking tests in school districts other than their own all the time. I'd like to see students be forced to take a test within a 30-mile radius of their high school. In general, when a kid doesn't make a score four times while taking a test in New Jersey and suddenly hits a home run and becomes a Rhodes scholar when taking the same test in California, it leads me to think there's some tinkering going on.

Then there are the kids who have no grades whatsoever — none — and everybody has known it for two or three years. But they're being promoted anyway.

I remember overhearing a conversation in an elevator during the summer of '98 after I had finished speaking to campers at the Adidas ABCD Camp in Teaneck, N.J. I was just riding in it and heard one kid ask another, "What about school, man? How are things going?" The other kid kind of shrugged his shoulders. "Oh, I'm not worried about grades. I'll just go to prep school and they'll take care of me."

How do kids with 1.5 GPAs go to a prep school and all of a sudden get all A's and become eligible to play without there being some sort of cheating going on? You see kids bouncing around in four or five high schools, then all of a sudden have the necessary credentials and are eligible. How does this happen? What's more, they want people to believe it's legit. No way.

Now, I have no problem with a kid who wants to go to a prep school because he wants to be a better all-around student, and maybe he wants to get away from an environment where he can't study. But I'm talking about the kid who becomes the hired gun. He bounces from school to school until he finds the right mix. I think what's happening here is you've got kids playing games. And if the eligibility formula becomes less weighted with the test scores, you'll alleviate all that.

When my daughters, Sherri and Terri, were in their junior year of high school I knew they would be heavily recruited because of their success in tennis. I did everything I could to help them improve their standardized test scores to better their chances of getting into top echelon schools. I paid thousands of dollars for tutors and special exam-preparation classes and both of them ended up landing full rides to Notre Dame.

Now, I ask you, does a kid from a struggling family have the same opportunity? No. And that's just one reason why I say standardized tests aren't fair. There are a lot of kids out there with tremendous potential, but maybe they just don't fare well on standardized tests. We need to give those kids at least a chance to make it.

For many, being in college might be the first time they have their own room along with three quality meals each day. They'll have a chance to rub shoulders with other students, and believe me in time these students begin to prosper. Why should we deny these kids an opportunity just because they didn't meet a certain score on a standardized test when we all know that these tests do not accurately measure the true potential of these youngsters?

NCAA president Cedric Dempsey has had to deal with some enormous issues during his tenure at the NCAA. I have to believe he wants to do the right thing as far as student-athletes are concerned. Photo 7-1. facing page (AP Photo).

Rules and Regulations

The NCAA's practices should be adjusted
to meet today's changing times

It certainly wasn't Fort Sumter, but rumblings of secession were coming from south of the Mason-Dixon line. Duke coach Mike Krzyzewski said that college basketball needs its own governing body, one separate from other NCAA sports. He said schools are losing underclassmen to the NBA at an alarming rate and that college basketball is changing at a "torrid pace" with which the NCAA can't keep up.

"The game is played on a day-to-day basis," Krzyzewski said. "It must be governed on a day-to-day basis. That's the only way to really solve problems. Agents watch over our sport every day. They are always looking for an opportunity. But there's nobody in the NCAA watching us every day. I know it goes against the structure of the NCAA. The NCAA is not sport-specific. The rulebook is all encompassing. But the time has come to make a change."

I spoke at length with Coach K about this, and he said, "We ought to hand the reins to somebody like former Big East commissioner Dave Gavitt or former Georgetown coach John Thompson because they understand the everyday problems and needs of college basketball. The NCAA means well, but it really doesn't understand some of the situations with which we're dealing. We need a governing body that can take this game further in terms of marketing."

I think that's a great idea. But this much is certain, you can't just eliminate the NCAA. The association, founded in 1910, has been good for college athletics. But clearly basketball needs attention.

I like the idea of this governing body working hand-in-hand with the coaches and dealing with the NCAA on a regular basis. It would be a win-win situation for the game of basketball, the NCAA, the coaches and the players. Why not capitalize on the gifted talents we have out there who have been there and can offer some expertise?

Ideally, the NCAA is supposed to be the perfect marriage of sports and education. But the 1,026-school governing body has taken a beating in recent years by court cases, big money pressures and Title IX issues. It's not surprising. It's such an easy target. The NCAA has been involved in a number of high-profile lawsuits as of late, all basically questioning its right to self-governance.

Perhaps the most public of all involved a suit by basketball coach Jerry Tarkanian, which was settled for $2.5 million. It's been bloody at times, especially where Tarkanian has been concerned. The NCAA pursued him for some 25 years, eventually getting him to resign from the University of Nevada-Las Vegas over numerous accusations of recruiting violations, just when it looked like Tark was on the verge of creating a dynasty in the desert. That situation seemed to go on forever. Even after the NCAA settled, it couldn't make up for all the pain, suffering and embarrassment Tarkanian suffered.

I'm not going to get involved in who was right and who was wrong, but there are some out there who have personal vendettas and want to prove they're right no matter what. The NCAA was later hit with a $67 million court judgment over a rule restricting the earnings of some coaches. Many critics feel this is the beginning of the end of the NCAA as we know it.

The problem dates back to 1991, when the NCAA, in the midst of a cost-cutting period, wanted to dump the third assistant coach from the basketball staff. Retired Atlantic Coast Conference commissioner Gene Corrigan thought he had a solution that would save the position and sold the NCAA on the idea of a restricted earnings coach (REC). Under the restricted earnings rule, each sport could have an assistant coach limited in pay to $16,000 a year — $12,000 during the academic year and $4,000 in the summer. Football was excluded.

But some coaches, including Duke's then-assistant Pete Gaudet, sued. Gaudet claimed he had a personal services contract with Mike Krzyzewski, in effect long before the REC was created, that paid him well above the limit, and on top of that he was paid handsomely for running the school's summer camp.

The rule was lifted in 1995 after the courts found that the NCAA violated antitrust law. The roughly 2,000 coaches involved then sued for back pay and won big, earning a $67 million judgment in 1998 from a federal judge in Kansas City. Later on, the judge in the case granted the coaches' motion to increase the damages to nearly $75 million to compensate for inflation.

The NCAA lost the appeal of that summary judgment in the 10th Circuit Court of Appeals, and its petition to have the U.S. Supreme Court hear the case was denied. The suit was finally settled for $54.5 million as a result of mediation service provided by the 10th Circuit Court of Appeals. The big problem now is how the money will be paid. If all Division I schools paid equally, the price tag would be $176,000 per school. That might not hurt the big schools, but it would kill the budgets of smaller schools. The small schools want the payments to be prorated according to what each school received from the NCAA and the CBS TV deal.

After the verdict, there was speculation that the larger programs might splinter off and form a super division. Nobody knows how reorganization might affect the basketball tournament, especially where non-football schools like Georgetown are concerned.

I thought the restricted earnings rule was invalid from day one. The idea that a coach can be limited to earning "X" amount of money is absurd. You can't expect a grown man on campus to live with the dollars they put out there. Everybody knew those guys weren't part-time workers. They were putting in hour after hour. So I commend guys like Peter Gaudet for fighting and making that happen.

I'm not ready to say the NCAA should be shelved. I just wish it had more bodies and a more consistent implementation of the 499-page Division I Manual, which needs to be rewritten, so there are no misinterpretations. In fact, I think the NCAA sometimes gets unfairly ripped; it's only trying to enforce the rules that are decided upon by the schools themselves. All schools have a say at the annual convention, and they determine what rules will be part of the NCAA.

The odds are against the NCAA when it comes to the governance and maintenance of all the rules. It simply doesn't have the manpower to be able to make sure everyone is playing by the rules. I've always felt it's done a pretty good job of letting schools know that there is little wiggle room once the NCAA's sights are locked onto an infraction.

In the summer of 1999, fewer than 100 people worked in the NCAA office, which relocated from the Kansas City suburb of Overland Park to Indianapolis. Only 35 percent of the 277-member staff chose to relocate. Unfortunately, there aren't enough investigators to handle all the calls they're getting regarding violations. Remember, member institutions are basically calling in with these inquiries, saying school "X" is violating this rule here, that rule there.

"It's a real challenge to try to keep the service going with the number of people we've lost," NCAA president Cedric Dempsey said. "We have a huge training effort to go through right now."

It's not only the staff that's in flux. There are always rumors floating around that the top 40 to 50 schools from the Big Ten, SEC, Pac-10 and Big 12 — which produce most of the revenue — will break away and form their own Division IV, in which they can make their own rules in recruiting, scheduling and distribution of profits.

Right now, it seems like everybody wants to join Division I just to share in the basketball tournament profits. The big schools still get more revenue units, based on conference performance in the Tournament, but the distribution is still watered down because there are more than 300 schools with various budgets.

There is little question about how important the NCAA Tournament has become to everyone involved. I'd just like to see some subtle changes. Some people say that by expanding the Tournament two weeks and including every school in Division I in the draw, maybe we can eliminate situations where expected teams get left out of the 64-team field.

Campus Chaos

In its quest to be the amateur sports capital of the world, Indianapolis lured the NCAA from surburban Kansas City to its newly constructed mega complex (foreground). Photo 7-2. (courtesy *Indianapolis Star*).

My feeling? Absolutely no. I'm totally against that for this reason: I think there's a certain mystery on selection day when you find out who's in. In essence, everybody has a shot at the NCAA Tournament.

Every league, with the exception of the Pac-10 and the Ivy League, has a conference tournament. Win the conference tournament and you earn an automatic bid to the Big Dance. It takes a special team to win six games in the NCAA Tournament. In the early rounds, there might be some upsets.

But when push comes to shove, check out the winners in the '90's: UNLV, Duke twice, North Carolina, Arkansas, UCLA, Kentucky twice, Arizona and Connecticut. It's the " crème de la crème" that has cut down the nets.

I have no problem with the selection process. It's now at a point where the committee has guys involved with basketball backgrounds, guys who understand what it's all about. In the past, there were some questions about match-ups. They say they use the computer, but you see certain match-ups, like Temple vs. Cincinnati, pop up over and over and you say, "How could that happen so many times?"

But I thought C.M. Newton and his people did a great job of selection and seeding in the 1999 Tournament. The only thing that bothered me was that I didn't understand the logic of picking the University of Alabama at Birmingham over Cal and Xavier. Cal had beaten UCLA, North Carolina, DePaul. But that's my own feeling. I'm against teams that don't have at least a .500 record in their conferences getting into the Tournament.

People say, "Well, they're in a tough conference." A school has the right to pick its league, but it should be competitive. Every conference should be included in the field. I like the idea of the little guy getting a chance to match up with the big guy because the big guy dodges him during the regular season.

Campus Chaos

When I coached at the University of Detroit, I was always looking to play top-25 teams. But they'd do it only on their terms, on their court. Dean Smith had a tradition at North Carolina of bringing his star players back home to play. Carolina out-recruited us for 6-11 Tommy La Garde from Detroit, so Dean called to see if we would play North Carolina in Detroit in exchange for two road games to North Carolina.

Well, I guess I can fess up to Dean now, but I was so excited just to be on the phone with him. We agreed to schedule those games, but I was lucky that I went on to the NBA and never had to make the journey down Tobacco Road with my Titans. The fact is simple, if you want to play the big guys, you have to play them on their terms.

I'm a big believer in teams getting to play Tournament games at neutral sites. I didn't like the idea of UConn having to play North Carolina at Greensboro in the 1998 Eastern Regional final. Nobody can tell me Carolina didn't have an advantage.

Billy Packer and I both like the idea of reseeding the teams once they get to the Final Four —1 to 4 — so that fans get a chance to see the best match-up in the championship game. Sometimes it seems the best games are in the semifinals. Duke vs. UConn was an exception. The NCAA must have done something right.

Hey, the organization has taken strides to overcome some of its shortcomings and over the past several years has been restructuring itself to better serve its members. The long-standing policy of "one school-one vote" legislation was tossed out the window, meaning Alcorn State no longer had the same voting power as Kentucky.

Now there's more autonomy within each of the three NCAA Divisions. In Division I, school presidents sit on a 15-member board of directors, each representing a conference. Athletic directors still develop legislation among others, but the board makes final decisions.

The NCAA, which budgeted $3 million for legal costs this year, plans to ask a law firm specializing in antitrust cases to review its rules. For good reason. A number of its rules and regulations have been drawn out into the court of public opinion for ridicule.

Especially troubling is a proposed new rule allowing full scholarship student-athletes to hold jobs during the academic year but capping pay at $2,000. In the past, athletes had been barred from such jobs. I'm all for kids being paid a stipend, but there have to be limits. If there aren't, it could tempt schools or boosters to line up high-paying jobs to lure athletes to their campus. That's a no-no.

The organization may be learning a lesson from its losses. Is a kinder, gentler NCAA on its way? Some recent cases might lead one to believe so. In the early spring of 1999, the NCAA overturned a postseason ban for the first time, giving Louisville's basketball team a chance to play in the 1999 NCAA Tournament. An appeals committee cited "procedural error" in the case of NCAA violations by former Louisville assistant coach Scooter McCray.

It said Louisville and McCray had not been adequately warned about the seriousness of the violations and that may have altered their defense before the NCAA. Louisville did not appeal its other penalties, including a three-year probation and loss of three scholarships. In pretrial hearings, Louisville interpreted the principal violation in the case — that Scooter McCray presented a credit card to guarantee the hotel bill to be paid by Fred Johnson, father of Cardinal forward Nate Johnson — as being secondary in nature.

The school maintained that it defended itself on that basis only to learn from the committee on infractions that the postseason ban was imposed because the Cardinals were repeat offenders. Louisville was already on probation because of former player Samaki Walker's use of a car in 1995. The school didn't argue the point because of the information it received from NCAA investigator Rich Hilliard, but it became

169

Louisville coach Denny Crum was the beneficiary of the first ever NCAA reversal of a post-season ban, allowing the Cardinals to play in the 1999 NCAA Tournament. Photo 7-3 (courtesy of University of Louisville)

the crux of the infractions committee's assessment of severe penalties.

Louisville was deemed a "repeat violator" and received a postseason ban. McCray, who was reassigned as a special assistant to AD Tom Jurich, won a separate appeal but eventually left the school in June 1999 after his contract ran out.

The NCAA said the former assistant also had not been adequately warned and lifted the requirement that any school wanting to hire him needed NCAA permission. In August, Hilliard said the enforcement staff didn't consider Louisville a repeat violator because he didn't consider the violations major.

But McCray is currently taking the NCAA to court, claiming his inability to get a coaching job was due to fallout from the investigation. His lawyer, Gregg Hovious, said the NCAA's re-evaluation of the case against McCray and Louisville had not changed perceptions about McCray. "Even though we believe in large part the NCAA exonerated Scooter of the allegations, it turns out ... people across the country in college basketball continue to believe he was somehow, frankly, a cheat."

In another case, the NCAA ruled that the Indiana football team would not be punished after coaches visited a recruit following the unexpected death of his father. Kris Dielman of Troy, Ohio, who signed a letter of intent to attend IU, called coach Cam Cameron following his father's death.

Cameron visited Dielman immediately after hearing the news. The contact was the second of the week for Cameron and Dielman, which, according to the NCAA, constituted a penalty. Also, assistant coach Jeff Hammerschmidt attended Michael Dielman's funeral, which placed one more coach on the road than was allowed during the particular recruiting period. The NCAA had originally ruled the actions constituted rules violations and levied several penalties, including ruling Dielman ineligible to compete at IU.

Maybe these cases show that the NCAA is starting to use some common sense. One of the problems with the rulebook is that there are a lot of rules that border on insanity and not logic. I figure it owes Indiana one, anyway.

Years ago, Steve Alford, an All-America guard at Indiana on the 1987 national championship team, was suspended from the Indiana-Kentucky game that year by the NCAA for posing gratis for a poster to benefit a charity. To me, that's insanity. What did he do to gain an unfair advantage for his school? Who was he hurting? But once again, the NCAA was merely reacting to legislation that has been passed by member schools.

Here's yet another recent example of a well-intended, but misused, rule actually hurting a kid instead of helping him. Aleksandar Radojevic, a 7-3 center from Barton County Community College in Kansas, signed with Ohio State for the 1999 school year. The best big man in junior college last season, Radojevic could have helped Jimmy O'Brien's team back to the Final Four.

But his background did him in. Radojevic is a rural kid from Montenegro, part of the former republic of Yugoslavia. Montenegro's economy has been ruined by ten years of war in the Balkans, so when Radojevic was in high school he accepted $13,000 to play for a local club team. Radojevic played only 19 minutes because he was so raw, and he gave all the money to his family.

He did not speak English and had no idea of the NCAA rules when he came to this country. Radojevic became a force in the game during his freshman year in junior college. He had grown into a 7-footer, and his former club team wanted him to return home. When Radojevic, who was concerned about being drafted into his native country's army, passed on the offer to return, he claimed the team blackmailed him.

"They said if I didn't come back I would never play basketball again," Radojevic said.

Radojevic believes club officials then dialed the number of the NCAA, which had no choice but to rule him ineligible. Radojevic then realized he had no choice but to be drafted — either by the Montenegrin army or by the NBA. He was the first big man selected in the 1999 draft — at No. 12 by Toronto. Another case of the NCAA's loss is the NBA's gain.

The kid wanted to play Division I basketball here. He should have been given the chance. Had the NCAA felt he deserved some penalty for accepting the money, it could have disciplined him by making him sit out some games, and reimburse, over his two-year period, some part of the fee he'd earned.

Radojevic was innocent in this situation. I thought the penalty was too severe. These kids don't know any of the intricate rules that exist out there, and many of them are penalized so unfairly. I think you have to look at a kid's intention. Did he intend to deliberately violate a rule and try to do something in a calculated way? In Radojevic's case, no.

It's the old motto "KISS'... Keep It Simple, Stupid." If guys are buying players, are flat-out cheating or participating in academic fraud, get them the heck out of the game. But in the case of Indiana, Alford or Radojevic, you shouldn't even have to talk about being lenient.

Conversely, the NCAA placed Cal State-Fullerton on four years' probation in April 1999 and restricted the school from offering scholarships to junior college transfers for three years. The reason? The infractions committee said that during the summer and fall of 1993 and summer of 1994, several prospective players who had enrolled in junior colleges received assistance with registering and paying the costs of correspondence courses at other institutions. According to the NCAA, the prospects allegedly received assistance in course registration at junior colleges and payment of tuition costs, in addition to improper cash payments, lodging, transportation and other benefits.

Every situation is different. There's no question the most severe penalty is the one that prohibits postseason play. But that should be reserved only for those who have cheated in a deliberate manner; buying players, academic fraud or gambling. But I can't see taking a school and barring it big-time for a minor violation.

I also have a real problem with the time it takes to hand down a penalty. In many cases, the coach is replaced, leaving the new coach to suffer the consequences. New players come in and suffer, too. I wish there were a way to issue penalties to those who committed the violations no matter where they move to and not issue them to those who had no intention to defraud.

But for all the debate about rules, regulations and NCAA standards, perhaps no single piece of legislation has affected collegiate athletics as much as the federally mandated Title IX. Created in 1972, Title IX prohibits sexual discrimination in institutions that receive or benefit from federal funds. Back then, women's sports at most universities were an afterthought to the men's programs.

Many sports have blossomed, but none more so than soccer. Women's soccer participation has grown 120 percent between 1990 and 1996. We see the results everywhere. Coaching has gotten better at every level. The teaching has gotten better. And the women have finally been taken seriously. In years past, female sports were thought to be merely recreational pastimes or amusements in the eyes of many. But today's female athletes are determined to become special players in every sport.

Was July 10, 1999, a watershed moment in women's sports in America? If so, heroes now have names like Mia, Brandi, Tiffeny, Tisha and Briana. Before the women's World Cup began, they were relative unknowns. After the U.S. national soccer team defeated China, 5-4, on penalty kicks following a 0-0 tie through 120 minutes, they had become icons. A crowd of more than 90,185, the largest ever to attend a women's sporting event, showed up to watch the game at the Rose Bowl in Pasadena.

President Clinton was there, along with 2,100 members of the media. I thought it was unbelievable. It created a real sense of pride. It was more than just soccer. It was red, white and blue. I'm going to be very honest, I don't know a thing about soccer. I don't know the rules, what happened in terms of overtime, double OT and the special kicks at the end.

But I was so excited about the emotion and the passion those young ladies were playing with that I caught the fever. What this team has done for the growth of soccer is just amazing. I think anybody who was watching it knew it was about America, the USA. And to see quality girls playing with no ego, playing as a team — that was absolutely beautiful. Briana Scurry and Mia Hamm. They are real "PTPers"... Prime Time Performers.

TV ratings went through the roof. The final was the most watched soccer game ever on U.S. network TV, with ABC estimating an audience of more than 40 million. The game posted an 11.4 national rating and a 32 share for the network.

The celebration started on the field when Brandi Chastain, who made the game-winning penalty kick — with her left foot — spontaneously ripped off her jersey, twirled it around her head, dropped to her knees and screamed before being mobbed by her exuberant teammates.

It continued the next day with a parade down Main Street at Disneyland and a rally in downtown Los Angeles, where the players were told their bonuses, originally set at $12,500, would be increased to $50,000 each. Then it was on to New York City for a tour of network morning shows like "*Good Morning America,*" "*Today*" and CNN and Fox News.

There was a midtown rally in Manhattan and a guest appearance at the WNBA All-Star game at the Garden. There was a book in the works about Mia Hamm and plenty of

Nobody does it better on the sidelines than Pat Summit of Tennessee. As you can see by Tennessee's six women's NCAA titles. Could she be the first woman to coach a men's team? I'd give her a shot. Photo 7-2. (courtesy of Patrick Murphy-Racey).

endorsements, a victory tour and the growing possibility of a women's professional soccer league.

The team passed the litmus test of sports fame in America: It appeared on a Wheaties box. This is the very best of what Title IX has brought us. I think the success of the women's soccer team is going to really translate into other sports, whether it be softball, field hockey, golf or basketball.

The 1999 WNBA All-Star game sold out at the Garden. My buddy Richie Adubato, who coaches the WNBA's New York Liberty, told me coaching women is an absolute joy. He told me the players have such a thirst for knowledge and they want coaching. They're not always moaning and groaning like many of the NBA superstars. Believe me, Richie knows as he's been a coach in the NBA with the Pistons, Mavericks and Magic. He said he's having fun again. Men coach women's college teams successfully as well. Look at Geno Auriemma of UConn and Leon Barmore at Louisiana Tech.

But you know what my final test for Title IX is? When will we see the day a college hires a female coach for a men's team? I can tell you one coach in basketball I'd give the job to, Pat Summitt of Tennessee. She's won six national championships. She's brilliant on the sidelines. I see a lot of competiveness in her, a lot of fire. She could coach on any level.

But with the identity, visibility and success the women's game is experiencing today, would she want to do it? Why be a pioneer just for the sake of being a pioneer? In any job, the bottom line is what a candidate brings to the table. If a coach can make a program successful, he or she should be hired.

If there's a woman who feels she wants to make that transition, and an athletic director who wants to give her an opportunity, so be it. But I don't think there is a woman out there who would want the hassle, even Pat Summitt. If you approached her and said, "We'll pay you mega dollars to coach a men's team," my gut feeling is she says no.

The scholarship opportunities today for women are awesome. Talk about these tennis academies. I used to tell Nick Bollettieri that everyone talks about the one or two who go on to make it professionally — Monica Seles, Jennifer Capriati — but that doesn't tell half the story. How about those who get college scholarships like my daughters did at Notre Dame?

The bottom line is that many of these players are going to go back and coach. And all of that will lead to more and more girls getting involved in sports, even in non-traditional ones, like football.

In 1999, a federal appeals court reinstated the sex discrimination lawsuit of Heather Sue Mercer, a female placekicker who was cut from Duke's football team in 1996. The court ruled that Mercer is entitled to a trial on her claim that Duke violated Title IX.

The unanimous decision reversed a ruling by U.S. District Judge N. Carlton Tilley, Jr. of Durham, who agreed that Duke could bar her from playing a contact sport, but that once she was allowed to participate Duke could not discriminate.

Mercer kicked the winning 28-yard field goal in Duke's 1995 spring scrimmage, and coach Fred Goldsmith publically told reporters she had made the team. She was listed on the official roster and pictured in the media guide. But she never kicked in a regular-season game as she was cut prior to the '96 season.

Mercer claimed Goldsmith's decision was based on gender because other, less qualified walk-on kickers were allowed to remain on the team. She claimed that Goldsmith made offensive comments to her, asking why she didn't prefer to participate in beauty contests instead of football games.

Along those same lines, Michigan State interim AD Clarence Underwood was chastised for making sexist remarks about female athletes in June 1999. "Women don't usually go out for sports because they love the sport,"

Underwood said. "Men go out for football, for example, because they love the game. Women go out for sports because of a scholarship."

Is there a negative to Title IX? It seems so. An NCAA report in 1998 found gender quotas are denying more than 20,000 men a chance to compete in college athletics compared to the 1992 rates, yet fewer than 6,000 female athletes were added. The Women's Sports Foundation has gone on record saying it is not in favor of reducing athletic opportunities for men as the preferred way of achieving Title IX compliance. A WSF study showed that between 1978 and 1996, Division I-A and I-AA have netted a total loss of 152 men's sports programs, an average of 8.4 per year.

But it happens. At Miami of Ohio, students had to say adios to the men's wrestling, soccer and tennis teams. Their supporters failed to raise $13 million in 70 days, the school's condition for keeping the teams, which it claimed it could not afford otherwise.

The golf team was able to raise enough money and was spared. Yet the university had enough money to elevate the women's precision skating team from club status; all because the school was under the gun to increase the proportion of female athletes by any means possible.

Elsewhere, Providence College had to disband its men's baseball team. In October 1998, Providence's president, the Reverend Philip A. Smith, announced that baseball, along with men's golf and tennis, would be eliminated from the varsity athletic program.

The cuts were made to comply with gender equity and proportionality rules set down by the NCAA and driven by the Federal Office of Civil Rights. Enrollment at Providence is 59 percent women and 41 percent men, yet 52 percent of the athletes are men. At Providence there are now nine women's sports to go along with nine men's varsity sports.

Nationally, women constitute 53 percent of Division I undergraduates but only 40 percent of the athletes. Providence's baseball team made its departure memorable, winning the Big East by beating St. John's, 6-1, to earn a bid to the NCAA Tournament.

"Going out in style is much better than just going out," head coach Charlie Hickey said. "We wanted to throw something back in the faces of the administration and prove to them what a mistake they made," said pitcher Marc Desroches. The team had been around for 78 years. You hate to see something like that happen.

Certainly, Title IX has a lot of positives. It's really helped women make great strides. But you hate if other programs have to pay. What blows my mind is when they talk about Title IX and want to count 85 football scholarships into the mix. You're not fielding a women's football team. If that's the case, it's not fair.

Some men are fighting back. At Cal State Bakersfield, the men's wrestling team was told it would have to cut its members to 30 due to Title IX. The players filed a suit so they could field an unlimited amount and won its preliminary hearing, their lawyer successfully arguing that gender-based cuts violate Title IX. The suit is scheduled to go to court in October 1999.

And it's not just the athletes. In June 1999, the U.S. Equal Employment Opportunity Commission ruled that the University of Pennsylvania committed gender discrimination in 1997 by denying Andrew Medcalf, an assistant men's crew coach, an interview for the then-open position of head coach on the women's team. Medcalf, who had been an assistant coach on the men's team for nine years, said he was qualified and that it was his gender that kept him from being considered.

In his complaint, Medcalf stated he had been told by an athletic department administrator that Penn intended to hire a coach who could "serve as a strong female role model" to the team — in particular, a woman who would be "at least as good if not better" than Medcalf. The Quakers hired Barb Kirch, an alumnus who had been women's crew head coach at Dartmouth for nine years.

Will there ever be equality among men's and women's coaches? A Women's Sports Foundation report, using 1995-96 data, found that coaches who head women's teams in NCAA Division I-A make 63 cents for every dollar earned by coaches who head men's teams.

And some coaches are slapping their schools with a technical because of it. Furman women's basketball coach Sherry Carter has filed a complaint with the Equal Employment Opportunity Commission, saying she should receive equal pay with men's coach Larry Davis. If the commission decides to pursue the complaint, it will attempt mediation.

A San Francisco federal appeals court turned down a suit by Cal-Berkeley coach Marianne Stanley, who sought equal pay with men's coach George Raveling when she was at USC. Stanley contended that the disparity in their salaries reflected the university's treatment of the women's program.

But the court, in a 2-1 ruling, said it wasn't necessary to decide whether the job duties of the men's coach were more demanding, because evidence showed that Raveling was more experienced and qualified than Stanley.

Raveling, according to published reports, was paid between $130,000 and $150,000 in 1993, when Stanley rejected the university's offer of a three-year contract for $96,000, a $26,000 raise. She wanted a contract that would bring her up to Raveling's level. When USC AD Mike Garrett refused, Stanley sued him and the school for $8 million.

The appeals court refused to reinstate her in a 1994 ruling. Stanley was unable to get a coaching job for more than two years and eventually was hired as promotions director at

Stanford, where she later helped coach before landing the Cal job in 1996.

When USC hired Raveling in 1986, he had 24 years of coaching experience, had been an assistant on the men's Olympic team, had been named National Coach of the Year and had years of marketing and promotional experience, the court said. Stanley had been a coach for fewer years and had none of Raveling's credentials.

Stanley's attorney, Robert L. Bell, pointed out that Stanley had won win three national championships at Old Dominion. She also played on two national championship teams at Immaculata. "It's like saying the women's experience doesn't count as much as the men's experience," he said. Obviously, every woman is entitled to make what she can.

But I think you're looking at two different situations. The pressure to survive and the pressure to meet the standards that are out there for men's coaches are greater than for the women's coach. Sure, every women's coach has pressure. But I think even the coaches who work the sidelines in women's college basketball would agree that the scrutiny is a lot more intense in the high-profile men's programs.

I don't think there should be a set number. Should Gail Goestenkors, the women's coach at Duke, make the same dollars as Mike Krzyzewski? Maybe in salary they're close, but Mike's certainly going to make a heck of a lot more in terms of outside revenue.

Each situation is unique, and each situation should be evaluated on an individual basis. In my mind, it's up to the discretion of the administration to award salaries based on the success of the program.

Should Pat Summitt make more than the men's coach at Tennessee? I wouldn't have a problem with that. She has been so successful, why not?

The women's game has made tremendous strides. This year, more than 300,000 attended the women's NCAA

Tournament. For the third straight year, Tennessee led the nation in home attendance and set a record for per-game attendance with an average of 16,565 spectators at Thompson-Boling Arena.

Connecticut was second with a 10,863 average, and Purdue was third with a 9,681 average. Several teams set single-game attendance records, topping 20,000. The Tennessee-UConn game on January 3, 1998, drew 24,597 in Knoxville; quite a change from the first women's NCAA championship that drew only 9,531 people.

During the 1998-99 season, ESPN and ESPN 2 televised all 52 games, including the entire Tournament. In 1982, the first year women's basketball appeared on ESPN, only five games were televised.

But there's still room for improvement. I think it's totally unfair for the women to play back-to-back games, on Saturday and Sunday, of their Final Four. Something should be worked out so that their Final Four can be held a week later, or earlier, than the men's so they can have the spotlight all to themselves.

They deserve their own moment in the sun. Now the real question remains: How much longer will the NCAA continue to have its place in the sun without getting burned?

Campus Chaos

John Thompson, who won an NCAA championship at Georgetown in 1984, was a pioneer for African-American coaches in college basketball. The big guy left huge shoes to fill after he resigned Jan. 8, 1999. Photo 8-1. facing page (AP Photo).

184

8

Best Man for the Job

It's about time more African-Americans are
hired as coaches for all college sports

At 6-10, 300 pounds, John Thompson was a towering figure in college basketball. Thompson, who unexpectedly resigned as coach of Georgetown University in January 1999, was one of the original Big East coaches, and his legacy is impressive: 596 wins, six Big East titles, three trips to the Final Four and one national championship.

In June 1999, Thompson was voted into the Basketball Hall of Fame. But as gaudy as his statistics may be, Thompson is known more for opening the door to opportunity for both coaches and economically deprived student-athletes. He made sure education came first. His first hire at Georgetown was Mary Fenlon, whose job was to oversee the players' academics. Some 97 percent of the players who spent four years in his program left with degrees, whether or not they had entered with academic qualifications. Those who weren't doing the job in the classroom after their first two years were invited to transfer.

His players learned their X's and O's too. He was the first African-American coach to win an NCAA title, and he became a hero, particularly in the African-American community. In addition, John broke the color barrier at Georgetown, attracting African-American players to a program that was mostly white when he arrived in 1972. He inherited a 3-23 team and built Georgetown into a national power. As a result, he had access to political giants and the ability to change NCAA legislation single-handedly.

He was never afraid to take a strong stand. According to *The Washington Post*, he successfully summoned an alleged drug kingpin, Rayful Edmond, now serving a life sentence in prison, to his office in 1989 and told him to stay away from two of his players, Alonzo Mourning and John Turner. Mourning, who was raised in a foster home with 35 children, has since gone on to make first-team All-NBA with the Miami Heat.

On ABC's "*Nightline*," Ted Koppel asked Thompson why he was philosophically opposed to Proposition 48. Thompson said he felt the college boards were culturally biased against African-Americans and said he was against using tests to determine eligibility for athletes. He gathered support from administers of the SATs and ACTs who also were opposed to using standardized tests as one of the two main criteria for determining eligibility and admission of athletes.

And Thompson was livid when the Southeastern Conference sponsored Proposition 42, because it made students who did not meet the minimums of a 2.0 GPA and either a 700 SAT or a 15 ACT score ineligible for financial aid.

Thompson felt the legislation would have its biggest impact on minority students. So the day before Georgetown was to play Boston College on national TV at the Capital Centre in Landover, Md., on January 14, 1989, he called a press conference to announce his plans to walk off the court in protest.

Just before tip-off, he got up from his chair and walked toward the locker room ... to a standing ovation. He left the building and drove around the city, listening to the game on the radio. Thompson also decided to boycott the team's next game, at Providence, his trademark towel left hanging over an empty chair.

When John walked off the court in protest against Proposition 42, I respected him for doing something he believed in. The guy wasn't afraid to take a stand and fight for his beliefs.

His protest drew immediate reaction. Albert Witte, the president of the NCAA, and Martin Massengale, then the chairman of the NCAA's President's Commission, announced that they would recommend postponing the legislation until more study could be completed. The next year, the NCAA modified the proposal to allow students who were ineligible for athletic competition to at least receive institutional aid so they could continue their education.

Thompson was also supportive of the boycott talk that arose in the fall of 1993, when the Black Coaches Association

187

pushed hard to have those eligibility restrictions reconsidered.

I didn't agree with the idea of a boycott at all because I don't think you solve problems in that fashion. I think that when John walked off the court, he made a stand, but there was no boycott — kids went on to play.

I think solutions come through dialogue, by getting people to sit down and hammer out solutions. It's better to get things done through discourse than to walk out in that fashion. I was glad the boycott never became a reality. I think that would have been a major mistake. It would have turned off a lot of people.

Ultimately, the initial eligibility rules were amended to allow partially qualifying athletes to play with their teams, receive aid and subsequently earn back a fourth year of eligibility by graduating with their classmates. A big "W" goes to John Thompson on that one. Again, John was fighting for something that was real, something that was positive, and something that could really help a kid. And people appreciated it.

The day he announced his resignation, you could see such loyalty and love between the president of the University and John — and between John and his players, who stood tall for him. John has a lot of heart, and in a way, he's a gentle giant. I really mean that.

One of his greatest assets was that he blended his kids into a unit. He taught them to play unselfishly and to play hard. I always respected the fact that Georgetown lived by a doctrine that I always believed to be basketball's first commandment: Thou Shalt Compete. Georgetown always came to play.

It wasn't easy for John to give it up, but he was going through a divorce that had been difficult on his family and felt he needed to devote more time to his personal life.

Coaches like John Chaney, Nolan Richardson and former coach George Raveling called, trying to persuade him to take a sabbatical or reconsider. But John felt it was time to move on. He stayed on campus to make sure the transition went smoothly but never tried to interfere with his successor, Craig Esherick.

We talked on the phone the day he resigned. In our conversation, I said I might not have agreed with everything he did. I didn't agree with the way he sheltered players. I didn't agree with the way he wouldn't let the media talk to the kids. I didn't agree with the way he hid them when he went off to different practice sites and didn't let the press watch practices, etc.

But I loved how he made sure those kids went to class — and at Georgetown, baby, academically it's not cupcake city. He made sure those kids graduated. People may have questioned his team's execution in the half-court offense, but no one has ever questioned the effort of Georgetown teams. They played hard, played with intensity, with emotion.

One of the things I love about John Thompson is the relationship he maintained with his ex-players. Even today, you see admiration from guys like Dikembe Motombo, Alonzo Mourning and Patrick Ewing. You see a closeness, a fatherly respect, a love and admiration. And that I respect.

Following him as coach will not be easy. But Esherick has one thing going for him, he's been on the staff for 17 years and has the great support of everybody who's a John Thompson guy. It will be easier for him than it would have been for an outsider. That coach would really have had it tough.

But I will say this. There are certain city-oriented programs — Marquette with Al McGuire, St. John's with Lou Carnesecca, Georgetown with John Thompson — where the coach becomes so big that his personality becomes a reflection of the whole city, not just the school. He becomes a recognized name. His influence is felt throughout the university:

in interest in the athletic program, in fund-raising, in media coverage. Most of all, his influence is felt in the recruiting war.

Because of this, I think it's easier for a new coach to carve his own identity on a traditional campus than in a big-city school where the previous coach was a giant. The big-city school needs a coach with an unbelievably strong personality. If the coach doesn't have a powerful presence, it's very difficult for that school to thrive. I really believe that.

In one respect, however, John's sights were set beyond Georgetown. He had a national agenda. He provided opportunities for a lot of young African-American assistants to become head coaches. Previously, they had been isolated. They were hired primarily as assistants who could go into the African-American community and recruit. John changed that.

The success he had helped open doors for African-Americans — guys like George Raveling, Tubby Smith and Leonard Hamilton — who started getting significant head-coaching jobs across America. John Thompson won a national championship in 1984. Nolan Richardson of Arkansas won it all in 1994. Tubby Smith of Kentucky won in 1998. John Chaney of Temple has been to the regional finals three times. Mike Jarvis of St. John's got to the Final Eight in the 1998-99 season.

There are a lot of African-American coaches who have gone out there in college basketball and have done a phenomenal job. And John made this happen. He stood for what he believed in. He didn't back down even if it was going to hurt his image, and he truly believed in giving people opportunities. These will be his legacies.

I still recall one of the special phone conversations I had with John. He asked me, "You know why opportunities are important? I just look at my own personal life. If I didn't get an opportunity to go to Providence — because I was not a great student and obviously my basketball skills enabled me to get an athletic scholarship— I would never have been able to pass it on to my kids. At Providence I learned so much about life.

And did it work? My son, Ron, went to Georgetown; my other son, John III, went to Princeton; and my daughter Tiffany went to Brown. All three have received first-class, big-time educations all because somebody gave me a chance, an opportunity."

That's why he and guys like John Chaney have fought — and fought a battle that I believed in from day one — against the reliance on the SAT and ACT scores in college admissions because they're tilted against minority students.

Are the odds stacked against minority coaches too? It seems so. In April 1998, ESPN hosted a "town meeting" in Houston titled "Race & Sports: Running in Place?" which dealt with racial issues in sports. Thompson pointed out that some colleges that are quick to embrace African-Americans as star players wouldn't consider them for coaching positions.

In college basketball, African-Americans account for 85 of the 310 men's head-coaching jobs in Division I. That's 27 percent, still well below African-Americans' 60 percent representation among players. Recognition has taken so long that some of these guys are now considered elder statesmen.

Nolan Richardson played for Texas-El Paso in the '60's, when he was prevented him from rooming and eating with his white teammates. He got his start coaching a team of Mexican-Americans at Bowie High in El Paso and then had enough success — winning the junior college national title at Western Texas Junior College — that Tulsa gave him a shot. Richardson coached Tulsa to the NIT title his first year, in 1980, and made three NCAA trips in five years before Arkansas called in 1985. He was 44 at the time.

Richardson's first two years were tough as he caught heat from boosters and newspaper columnists in the state who didn't like the fact that he was the first African-American

Arkansas coach Nolan Richardson is among the most talented and succesful African-Americans in a major college head coaching position. And, he's the only active head coach with the President rooting for his team. Photo 8-2. (courtesy of University of Arkansas).

coach in the Southwest Conference. But he eventually turned it around with his "40 Minutes of Hell" style of play, making it to the Final Four in 1990 and winning the national title in 1994 with big plays from Scotty Thurman and the team that helped stop Grant Hill and Duke. It gave him a rare "trifecta"... a junior college title, an NIT title and an NCAA title.

Today, Richardson is still a fierce competitor, a scrapper. He's made out of the same mold as John Thompson. You may not agree with everything he says, but he's a guy who's going to tell you what he feels. He's going to come after you, and his teams reflect his personality. They come after you with an attacking style. When you count the number of W's in the '90's, Arkansas is right up there with all the top programs.

According to some, the Razorbacks slipped a little. But to me, Arkansas will always be a factor in the top 20 as long as Nolan is on the sideline. And what other coach can count a U.S. President as his biggest fan?

Another great coach, John Chaney, has Hall of Fame written all over him. Chaney spent ten years at Division II Cheyney State, where he won a national championship in 1978. But he didn't catch a break until 1982 when Temple, a school that passed him over for a scholarship when he was a senior in the Philadelphia Public League, gave him a chance.

Chaney's made the most of it, coaching the Owls to 15 NCAA Tournament bids in 17 years and four trips to the NCAA regional finals, in 1988, '91, '93 and '99. He's a tireless worker, and what he's achieved over the years at Temple is awesome.

A lot of guys say, "Oh, man, I'm tired of watching his antics on the sideline. He's screaming. He's yelling." Let me tell you something, the emotion and love he pours out in a game and the feelings and the teachings he conveys to his players are so special. Just go to one of his practice sessions

Temple's John Chaney deserves a spot in the Basketball Hall of Fame. He coaches the best match-up zone in the country and has replaced the late Harry Litwack, the wise old Owl, as the all-time winningest coach at that school. Photo 8-3. (AP Photo).

— at 5:30 in the morning. Watch how he's molding these kids into men.

Like Thompson, he has pushed for the rights of minority students. Chaney has been a staunch opponent of Proposition 48 and the use of standardized tests to determine eligibility. Some question Temple's graduation rate—just 9 percent, according to an NCAA survey that charted players who entered college in 1991-92 and were given six years to graduate.

But let's face reality—he's not getting the student-athletes who go to some of those so-called elite schools. He does an amazing job. I judge a coach by simply asking, "Is he getting the most out of the kids that wear his uniform and are they getting an education not only in the classroom and basketball court but also in the game of life?" At Temple, the answer is yes, and that's what John Chaney is all about. His teams' performances, over the years, have been unbelievably successful all things considered.

All most coaches need is somebody to give them a chance. Look at Tubby Smith at Kentucky. He won the national title in 1998 by getting a good team to play sensational basketball in March. Tubby came into a tough situation; replacing Rick Pitino at a school that had recently played in the NCAA finals and won the national championship the prior year.

When Rick left for a $50 million job with the Boston Celtics, C.M. Newton, the AD at Kentucky, showed why he's such a brilliant administrator. He acted swiftly and didn't play games. He didn't conduct a national search and allow the hiring game to become a circus. C.M. had one guy in mind all the time, and he went after him.

He didn't look to be a hero and say, "Wow, I want to hire the first African-American men's basketball coach in Kentucky." He simply wanted the best person to replace the legend, Rick Pitino. His guy was Tubby Smith.

Kentucky made history when it hired Tubby Smith, an African-American coach, to replace Rick Pitino. Smith went on to become a hero in the Commonwealth, cutting down the nets the next spring at the NCAA Finals in San Antonio. Photo 8-4. (AP Photo).

You know what was so beautiful about that? There was no consideration about the color of the applicant's skin. It was all about the best man for the job.

I like the fact that C.M. didn't allow himself to be used. He didn't act like so many AD's do, guys who let themselves be wheeled and dealed by coaches whose names pop up for this job or that job only because the coaches want more money at their current schools.

Tubby earned it. He had worked as an assistant coach at Kentucky and had been the head coach at Tulsa and Georgia, taking both programs to the Sweet 16. Now, with all the resources he inherited, he has a chance to start a dynasty in the Blue Grass.

I know there are some people in Kentucky who were upset with C.M. for hiring an African-American coach, but that's one of the things that makes C.M. so special. People were nervous about the pressure Tubby would be under by taking the job. But Pitino said it best in an interview, "Pressure is an ally. Stress is the enemy."

Tubby represents all that's good about coaching. He loves kids and cares about his players. I don't buy the talk that Ryan Hogan and Michael Bradley didn't feel wanted because Tubby hadn't recruited them. Basically, I think Tubby wants his players to produce.

I also think that maybe he felt a little guilty about trying to keep players happy. He was rotating a lot of bodies during the '98-99 season — Jules Camara, Jamaal Magloire, Michael Bradley and Scott Padgett. He was trying to get some PT for all these guys, to keep them happy so they wouldn't leave.

I don't think Tubby had to win a national championship to be accepted at Kentucky, but obviously it didn't hurt him either, baby. I remember doing a game at Kentucky with Brent Musburger a couple years ago when the Wildcats lost to Florida and Jason Williams, who could have won the award for best individual performance of any guard I'd witnessed that year. He went off for 24 points and dazzled a national TV audience. In fact, sitting next to me doing radio was former Wildcats star Sam Bowie, who told me Williams was the best guard he'd seen all year.

Brent and I were running out to get the car that would take us to the airport after the game. Man, we got to the lobby of the hotel connected to Rupp Arena, and we had fans screaming at us. One guy was saying, "If Rick was here, this wouldn't be happening." At the time, Kentucky had a super record, but the fans couldn't believe that they had lost at home to Florida. I said, "Wait a minute. Do you know what this guy's record is? He's lost about three games." And they're screaming about wanting Rick here.

I'd have liked to have seen that guy at the end of the year when the Wildcats cut down the nets and Kentucky won the national championship. I guarantee you he was running around, painted blue, saying, "Tubby's my man."

St. John's fans may feel the same way about Mike Jarvis. Jarvis got his start as Patrick Ewing's high school coach at Rindge and Latin in Cambridge, Mass. He got into college coaching at Boston University, then moved to George Washington University, where he took a program that was at the bottom of the Atlantic 10 and put it back on its feet.

In eight years, Jarvis coached the Colonials to a 152-90 record and five NCAA Tournament appearances. But he could never escape from the long shadow of Thompson's Georgetown program or that of nearby Maryland and the ACC, until now.

When Jarvis took over at St. John's for Fran Fraschilla in the spring of 1998, he not only inherited an excellent team, he also had a chance to be the top dog in the big city after playing third fiddle to Georgetown and Maryland while in Washington, D.C. It didn't hurt that he coached St. John's to the regional finals in his first year.

Not being an African-American makes it tough for me to talk about whether racism still exists in athletics. I don't have to deal with some of the problems that, unfortunately, many of my friends experience. But I believe that the one thing about sports — and college basketball, in particular — is that it's the one place in American society where a man is judged by his ability to perform and not by the color of his skin. No doubt there are some tunnel-vision individuals, black and white, who have their own bigoted beliefs.

But isn't it beautiful to watch a team celebrate a championship like UConn did in 1999, and you see players and coaches of different colors and religions hugging one another and celebrating the special moment together. The one thing college basketball can stand tall about is that it has really done a solid job of trying to close the gap that existed so many years ago.

And remember the guy who made it happen, the guy who really opened doors back in 1966, Don Haskins, who retired from Texas-El Paso in the summer of 1999. The school was called Texas Western back then. Haskins coached a team with five African-American starters to history when they beat top-ranked, all-white Kentucky, 72-65, to win the national championship at Cole Field House at the University of Maryland.

They destroyed the prejudice and myth that African-American athletes didn't play disciplined basketball. Haskins was one of the greatest disciplinarians the game has ever known. Here's a Hall of Famer who won more than 700 games, but he'll always be remembered for the way his under-sized team, featuring three starters 6-1 or shorter, frustrated Kentucky. How Bobby Joe Hill, one of the TW stars, converted two steals into lay-ups on back-to-back trips down the floor. I remember that team was very athletic, very physical, and very tough defensively.

To beat Kentucky made it even sweeter because of Adolph Rupp's reputation for dominating the national scene.

Kentucky was one of the giants of college basketball under Rupp. His teams had won four national championships, and everybody thought they couldn't lose — everybody but Haskins and those 12 kids from Texas Western.

That game had big-time impact. It was highly visible because it was played on national TV and gave people something to think about. It shook up people and made them think, "Wow, this hasn't happened before."

That's why I have such a problem with college football. Civil rights activists again are crying foul over a lack of minority hiring in major college football programs, where almost 51 percent of the athletes are African-American. Entering the 1999 season, only five of the 112 Division I-A (4.38 percent) coaches were African-American: Jerry Baldwin of Southwestern Louisiana, Jim Caldwell of Wake Forest, Tony Samuel of New Mexico State, Bob Simmons of Oklahoma State and Tyrone Willingham of Stanford. The first African-American coach in Division I-A was hired only 20 years ago.

As late as 1991, there were no African-American coaches in the division. Of the 54 head-coaching vacancies in the last three years, only two have been filled by African-American candidates. Only Baldwin was among the 20 coaches named in the most recent round of NCAA Division I-A hirings following the 1998 season. The year before, there was one African-American hired among 24 vacancies. In that same period, four African-American coaches had resigned or been fired.

Colorado was criticized in 1995 for hiring the less experienced Rick Neuheisel over longtime assistant Bob Simmons, an African-American who eventually got the head job at Oklahoma State. When Neuheisel left to coach Washington after the 1998 season, Colorado hired Gary Barnett from Northwestern.

"That's just unacceptable," says Rev. Charles Farrell of Rev. Jesse Jackson's Rainbow/PUSH Coalition. "We're not moving forward. We're actually moving backwards." The

Rainbow/PUSH Coalition has petitioned Congress for hearings into minority hiring practices in college football.

Critics of the NCAA feel the problem is not being addressed as it should. It wasn't even discussed during the 1999 NCAA Convention in San Antonio, which infuriated Rudy Washington, NCAA Management council member, commissioner of the predominately African-American SWAC, and former executive director of the Black Coaches Association. "Nothing is going to happen until the coaches decide to make a stand," says Washington.

I can't understand the logic of what's happening — or should I say not happening — in college football. It's been a nightmare. When I look at all the great African-Americans who have been playing the game over the years, it amazes me how few have become head coaches in college football. And the guys who have gotten jobs got them at Eastern Michigan, Louisville, Wake Forest and Temple, where coaches are automatically at a disadvantage because there's no football tradition, so recruiting is difficult.

College football needs a John Thompson, but it won't get him until more big-time programs start hiring qualified minority candidates. Come on now, let's get real here. Let's see somebody have the guts to hire the most qualified guy in a legit job where he's got a chance to win.

Sports are not supposed to be black and white, but there are times when it must seem that way, especially in the pros. Baseball Hall of Famer Joe Morgan pointed out during a special on ESPN that some of the greatest players in baseball history have been African-Americans, yet once they finish their careers, it seems there's no place for them to go.

Some of the facts are eye opening. According to the latest Race and Gender Report Card, issued by the Center for the Study of Sport in Society at Northeastern University, there were no African-American or Latin majority owners in any of the leagues studied — the NBA, NFL, MLB, NHL or MLS.

Former Cleveland Browns running back Jim Brown raised the stakes regarding minority ownership of a professional sports team by calling on wealthy African-American athletes to invest in teams. He wanted to know what celebrities like Michael Jordan and Tiger Woods were going to do with all that loot they're making, especially from Nike. Brown has suggested that Nike is getting far greater benefit from Jordan, Woods and Thompson than any of them are giving back to the African-American community.

John Thompson, however, says that what minority owners really need is the big money backing from major financial institutions, rather than that of individual athletes. No matter what you believe, you would have to say that such dialogue is definitely productive.

But while all this talk is moving us forward, moving us toward a day when we're all accepted for who we are and not for what color we are, there are too many sobering examples of how racism still breathes in America. During the summer of 1999, the news of the racially motivated death of one of my friends, former Northwestern basketball coach Ricky Byrdsong, shook me to the core. I still have trouble believing what happened.

While out walking with his two little children in the early morning on a quiet neighborhood street on the border of suburban Skokie and Evanston, Ill., Byrdsong probably never noticed the blue Ford Taurus pulling up behind them. Without warning, Byrdsong was shot in the back, allegedly by 21-year-old self-professed white supremacist Benjamin Smith. Byrdsong died on the way to the hospital.

Authorities said Smith had gone on an indiscriminate two-day shooting spree, targeting Orthodox Jews, African-Americans and Asian-Americans. He killed two, including Byrdsong, and wounded nine before taking his own life. Byrdsong was just 43. He left behind a wife, Sherialyn, and three children, Sabrina, 12, Kelly, 10, and Ricky Jr., 8.

202

It was so sad, so tragic, so wrong...some lunatic taking a gun and snuffing out the life of an innocent man because of racism. Byrdsong became another statistic in a year of senseless violence. I was watching TV a couple of days later, and one of the networks was actually showing film of Smith passing out literature that promoted hate. I'm all for freedom of speech, but give me a break—to me, preaching hate is a violation of what America is all about.

The shootings might have been racially motivated, but friends of mine who attended the funeral told me there were no color lines or religious differences in the First Presbyterian Church in Evanston the night of Byrdsong's funeral. Jewish, Muslim, Christian, Buddhist...more than 1,600 from all walks of life packed the church.

I vividly remember my meetings with Ricky because he had a smile that filled the room. My first meeting with him occurred when he was an assistant on Lute Olson's staff at Arizona. Then he coached at my old school, Detroit Mercy, before taking over the head-coaching job at Northwestern in 1993. Byrdsong lasted only four years at Northwestern before he was fired.

He took his first team to the NIT. But as a coach, he will be remembered as much for a point-shaving scandal about which he knew nothing and that strange night when a bizarre motivational stunt turned sour and he wandered through the stands, chatting with fans, at a Minnesota game.

But there is more to Ricky Byrdsong than just X's and O's. He was a deeply religious man, a good father and husband, a deacon in his church and head of community affairs working with inner-city kids at Aon, a multimillion-dollar insurance company in Chicago. He may have been a victim of racial hatred, but Byrdsong stood for racial reconciliation in death.

At the funeral, pastor Lyle Q. Foster of the Worship Center, Byrdsong's church, asked, "Why is it that a black man has to be shot before people realize his greatness?"

I'm told that the service was upbeat, filled with gospel music, which had many in the crowd on their feet, clapping and singing. But there was no mistaking the tragedy, from the grief-stricken looks on the faces of Byrdsong's children to the sadness in the eyes of his former players.

Just before the service started, Dion Lee, who had been convicted in the 1994 point-shaving scandal, walked up to the casket and broke down, collapsing into the arms of Shawn Parrish, one of Byrdsong's assistant coaches.

Then, as the three-hour service was about to end, Pastor Foster told this chilling story in his eulogy: A few days after the shooting, Sherialyn was talking to Ricky Jr., who had witnessed his father's murder, about what a great man his father was. "And you're going to be a great man someday too," she said. "Does that mean I'm going to get shot too?" Ricky Jr. asked.

I can only pray that society will become more tolerant in young Ricky's lifetime.

I still can't believe the way Iowa treated Dr. Tom Davis after all the years he gave to that Big Ten school. Davis, who was forced out by the administration, got the last laugh when he took his final team to the NCAA Sweet 16. Photo 9-1. facing page (AP Photo)

Blinded by Success

*Sportsmanship and loyalty has left college athletics,
replaced by the quest for W's*

Is there any honor left in college basketball? Doesn't
appear to be. It seems everywhere I look, programs are in a

state of conflict. And worse than that, I see less and less sportsmanship and more and more selfishness.

Look at what happened at Iowa. After 13 years as head coach, Tom Davis is pushed out by athletic director Bob Bowlsby, who replaced him with Steve Alford from Southwest Missouri State. Davis, whose teams won 20 games in each of the last five years and reached the Sweet 16 in 1999, ran into problems with Bowlsby, who tried to force him to retire at the end of the 1998 season after Davis failed to get Iowa into the NCAA Tournament.

Davis talked Bowlsby into letting him stay one more year, and Bowlsby bought into the compromise, but it backfired when Davis became a rallying point for a team of overachievers that made a run at the Big Ten title.

Bowlsby was disturbed by a continued dip in home attendance, was incensed that Iowa kept losing blue-chip in-state prospects like Raef LaFrentz, who went to Kansas, and remained haunted by what he perceived as Davis' unwillingness to discipline problem-child Chris Kingsbury in 1996 after an ugly elbowing incident against Penn State.

Bowlsby caught his share of backlash, but he refused to back off his decision to dump Davis. Davis refused to get caught up in the controversy and left quietly.

Tom Davis got a raw deal. I thought what Bowlsby did was totally unjustified and uncalled for. Yes, it's the university's prerogative to fire a coach and make a change. Every coach knows that going in. A coach is paid well, and if the school isn't happy with the job he's doing, fine. Bye-bye. But making Davis a lame-duck coach caused embarrassment to the university and the athletic department.

So there Davis was, marching on to the Sweet 16 after beating Arkansas in the second round. Supposedly he didn't even get a handshake from the athletic director or the administrative staff after the win. Tom Davis has always been a man of integrity on that sideline. He always had the best interest of the kids at heart and had a great track record at every school that employed him, whether it was Lafayette, Boston College, Stanford or Iowa. His treatment at Iowa was definitely second-rate.

Another coach, Fran Fraschilla, can sympathize with him, I'm sure. Fraschilla got a raw deal too, when St. John's fired him after a 22-win season. According to Fraschilla, St. John's was hurt that Fran was even talking to other schools that were knocking on his door in the summer of 1998 after he'd led the Red Storm to the NCAA Tournament in just his second year. According to Fran, he toyed with the idea of talking to a few, including Arizona State, but never did anything without getting permission from St. John's AD Ed Manetta. Still, his actions were considered an act of treason in the eyes of Rev. Donald Harrington, St. John's president, who promptly fired him. The price tag? St. John's had to pay off the final two years of his contract, which totaled $580,000. Hey, it's only money.

Harrington then went out and hired Mike Jarvis of George Washington, paying him $735,000 a year. Fran wanted to stay at St. John's, but school administrators decided — after watching him take St. John's to the NCAA Tournament and sign blue-chip prospects like Ron Artest and Erick Barkley — to pull the plug. In the end, though, St. John's made a great choice in hiring Jarvis.

When Jarvis arrived, there were questions about how he would deal with the players Fraschilla had recruited, but he did a terrific job managing talent like Artest and Barkley. He coached St. John's into the top ten and just missed getting to the Final Four, losing to Ohio State in the South Regional final. Fraschilla sat out a year and later resurfaced at New Mexico, where I'm sure he'll be a winner.

Other Big East programs have had their share of problems over the last few years as well. Jim O'Brien won the 1997 Big East Tournament while head coach at Boston College, but he and the school's admissions director were at

Fran Fraschilla got a rare second chance, resurfacing at New Mexico after being fired by St. John's. He had coached the Red Storm to 22 wins and an NCAA bid in 1998. Photo 9-2. (AP Photo)

odds after the university refused to admit two prospects, Elton Tyler and Jon DePina, even though both projected. O'Brien left BC in a huff and is still sore. But I'm sure the way he coached the Ohio State Buckeyes from the basement of the Big Ten into the semifinal game of the Tournament in 1999 will help him get over it.

Fraschilla and O'Brien were lucky to have so quickly bounced back from the Ziggy Club. Let's face it, a lot of guys-don't. We hear all the time about the coaches who make the million-dollar salaries, but we never talk about the guys who get the ziggies, as in fired. It's not easy being fired because everybody wants to talk about your last job. Nobody ever wants to talk about the positives you've added to your resume over the years.

O'Brien was fortunate that Ohio State AD Andy Geiger was willing to take a gamble. When O'Brien was hired, I thought Geiger had made a mistake because I felt that Jim, being a New Englander, would have difficulty adjusting to the Midwest. But it proves once again that where you're from matters less than your abilities. If you're a good coach, a good communicator, a hard worker and you run an honest pro-gram...you will win.

How wrong I was to think O'Brien wouldn't do it after Pitino had done it at Kentucky and Billy Donovan is doing it right now at Florida. It's all about communication, baby. That's what Jim O'Brien did. He took some punishment for a year, but Scoonie Penn transfered from Boston College and we've seen how the team took off. It went from 1-15 in the Big Ten to the Final Four. Jim O'Brien had the last laugh.

The Boston College basketball program deserves to be treated better by their school administration, and the guy who certainly deserves better is the coach there now, Al Skinner. All he wants is a chance to win. Does he get a chance with the restrictions the admissions department placed on him? Can he beat the likes of St. John's and

Connecticut? The schools in the Big East make it awfully difficult.

I say to Boston College, "If you want to play by different rules, then join the Ivy League, where there are no scholarships." That's fine. There's nothing wrong with that. I've said that in the past about schools like Northwestern and Rice in their conferences. If you're not committed to being competitive with the schools in your conference, don't let your kids go out there and get pounded week after week. Don't make your student body sit there and develop an inferiority complex about its team.

Some coaches don't agree with the "less is more" philosophy. Wichita State coach Randy Smithson was reprimanded for violating practice limits. His star player, Maurice Evans, who has since transferred to Texas, complained that players were demeaned and isolated by the staff. I spoke at Wichita State's preseason banquet in 1998, and chatted with Randy Smithson and met Maurice Evans. I never attended practice, but I'm sure there are situations in college athletics, as in any other profession, where sometimes, under the pressure to win, a coach might step over the line.

When I think back to my own coaching days — has it really been more than 20 years since I coached on the college level? — I know I made some mistakes. I remember being in the gym and putting my players through some punishing drills, just out of frustration. But I never went as far as Kevin Bannon did at Rutgers.

A story leaked last summer that in December 1997, Bannon organized a strip free-throw shooting contest in which players and managers removed an article of clothing any time they missed a foul shot. In the end, two players — Josh Sankes and Earl Johnson— and two managers were left totally naked and had to run the floor. Bannon, for his part, says no one was forced to participate and that he did it to break up the monotony of Christmas break. I gotta believe that Bannon wishes he'd never done it. Let's just hope it's all behind him and he grows from this mistake...just another fraternity hazing.

In every case, a coach's job is to get the most out of his athletes, get them to understand they can give so much more than they do. I think we underestimate the value of what a player is able to do, how much a coach can get from him. If you study the great coaches, you see they have an ability to get the most out of their talent because they're willing to take that extra step.

Speaking of taking steps, if a coach wants to leave early, I think it's up to the individual school if it wants to let him out of his contract. If a guy signs a multi-year deal to remain at a university, the administration assumes he'll stay.

Today, schools give five, six extensions to a coach's contract. Sometimes I wonder, "What are all these extensions? What are they about?" Schools laying on all these extensions, and guys are leaving after one year. The administration needs to be strong and put a clause in the contract stating that the school will collect a penalty fee if the coach leaves early. Simple as that.

There is so much importance placed on that coach being there. If a guy signs a five-year extension and then wants to leave, fine. But somehow, the school should be compensated for those years after he leaves. A school shouldn't want to keep a coach who doesn't want to be there. If a coach wants to go elsewhere, so be it, let him go.

But he should be held accountable for leaving. I really believe that. When a coach is hot, players feel the heat. And when other schools come after him, his current school is at his mercy. And sometimes more than once.

Rhode Island gave a big extension to Jim Harrick, and he pulled out to go to Georgia. Twice. But can you really blame Harrick? How many guys turn down a multi-year contract from an SEC school? Remember, Harrick won a national championship at UCLA and did one heck of a job at Rhode

Island. One can understand the disappointment at Rhode Island, but I think the people in the profession understand why he would take the Georgia job. Georgia came after Harrick hard last spring, offering him a contract worth more than $500,000 a year with an annuity that kicked in at the end of four years.

Harrick, who had coached Rhode Island to a pair of NCAA Tournament bids in the two years he was there, accepted the job, then changed his mind because of family considerations. He knew he couldn't take his son, Jim Jr., with him as an assistant coach because Georgia has a nepotism rule. And another son had just moved East to start a new business.

When Harrick got back to Rhode Island, both of his sons told him this was too good an opportunity to turn down. So he called Vince Dooley, the Georgia AD, and got on the next plane to Athens. His decision didn't make him very popular in Kingston, where the folks at Rhode Island had called a press conference to announce Harrick was returning.

It was the second time in three years that a coach had embarrassed Georgia by accepting a head-coaching job and then changing his mind. In December 1995, Glen Mason was hired from Kansas to coach the football team but changed his mind days later and returned to the Jayhawks.

College coaches are treated like CEOs of major corporations — and they should be. When you think of the revenue from ticket sales and merchandise they're bringing in, all the pressure they're under every day, these guys — giants like Mike Krzyzewski, Roy Williams, Lute Olson — should be paid handsomely. Ultimately, they're judged by a balance sheet of assets and liabilities —W's and L's.

Take Dave Bliss, for example. After 11 years in Albuquerque, Bliss left New Mexico for Baylor after the 1998-99 season. He was successful as the Lobos' head basketball coach but not successful enough. The Lobos were regular visitors to the NCAA Tournament during Bliss' 11 years there.

212

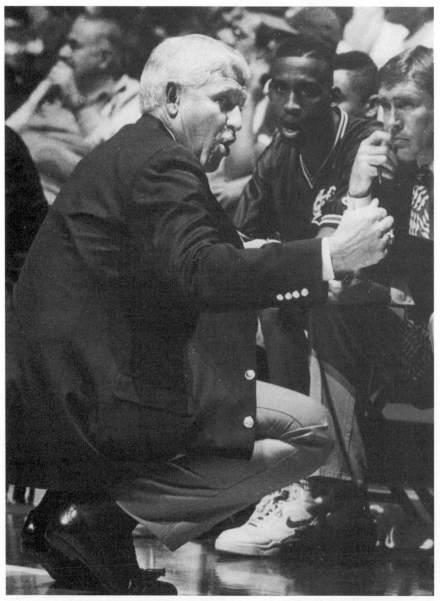

Like CEO's of major companies, marquee coaches such as Arizona's Lute Olson are constantly under great pressures to succeed. That kind of pressure and the big revenue they generate justify their big paychecks. Photo 9-3.   (courtesy University of Arizona)

They won 102 games in four seasons and were ranked in *The Associated Press* Top 25 for 54 straight weeks. But they rarely escaped the second round of the NCAA Tournament, not good enough for the fans at The Pit. Bliss was tired of the criticism, claiming the hardest thing he had to coach against in Albuquerque was the community. At Baylor, Bliss inherited a program that was 0-16 last year in the Big 12. But it was a fresh start.

It didn't take long for New Mexico AD Rudy Davalos to fill his spot with Fran Fraschilla. The money being tossed around is mind-boggling. San Diego State offered Rick Majerus of Utah a $1 million deal to rejuvenate the program there. He turned it down, but former Michigan coach Steve Fischer grabbed the ring. And Texas got Rick Barnes to leave Clemson for a multiyear deal worth $700,000 a year.

For some of these coaches, opportunity is all you want. A chance to vindicate yourself, to prove you can still win. For others, new jobs mean bigger expectations, like moving up from Triple-A to the big leagues. I'll tell you, it's hard to break into the Bigs.

When I coached at the University of Detroit, I would get so frustrated. I wanted to recruit the same way as Michigan, but in those days, Michigan's phone budget was bigger than my entire budget. Michigan was the Big Ten. I wasn't. I was so limited. I just couldn't jump on a plane and travel.

But for those marquee programs, just having a great regular season and getting into the Tournament isn't really what it's all about. The local writers who are banging the keyboards and the real die-hard fans want more. There is a bottom line for programs like UCLA, North Carolina and Kentucky. The only question their supporters have is, "What are you doing to get to the Final Four?" At least reaching the Final Four breaks the barrier and says, "Wow, you've really made it this year." And once a coach has made it there, everybody wants him. Or so it seems.

Utah's Rick Majerus is generally regarded as one of the best teaching coaches in the country. He's on everybody's A-List. Last spring, Notre Dame picked up the phone and dialed his number. Majerus met with Irish AD Mike Wadsworth. He showed real interest in the job. Wadsworth thought enough of Majerus to recommend him to the school administration.

Later on, stories surfaced that several administrators were upset about a passage in Majerus' book, *My Life on a Napkin*, in which Majerus said he would have difficulty disciplining one of his players for academic fraud because he had been guilty of cheating when he was an undergraduate at Marquette.

That was 30 years ago. Majerus has since become a firm academic disciplinarian. When Utah went to the Final Four in 1998, two of his players — Mike Doleac and Drew Hansen — were both academic All-Americans. Nine of his players made the Dean's list, and All-America guard Andre Miller, who came to Utah as a Proposition 48, graduated in four years and earned a fifth year of eligibility.

With Majerus out of the picture, Notre Dame eventually chose Matt Doherty, one of Roy Williams' assistants at Kansas, for the job. Doherty certainly has the pedigree. He's from New York, played for Dean Smith at North Carolina and was a starter on the 1982 national championship team that featured Sam Perkins, James Worthy and Michael Jordan, worked on Wall Street and was an assistant at one of the nation's elite programs.

More and more schools are reaching out to high-powered assistants to fill job vacancies. Missouri plucked Quin Snyder from Duke. Marquette went to Michigan State for Tommy Crean. Smart athletic directors know where to find a few good men. I think it's so positive when that happens. It's good to see new blood injected into a program.

I like to see guys being rewarded for being a vital part of a successful program. So many programs just recycle. Usually you don't move from an assistant to a major-college

Utah coach Rick Majerus is highly regarded for his ability to teach the finer points of the game to promising student-athletes. A shining example is recent graduate and all America guard Andre Miller who overcame academic challenges to graduate in four years. Photo 9-4. (courtesy of University of Utah).

head-coaching job. Unless you have guys like Dean Smith putting in a good word for you.

It happened at Kansas with Roy Williams. Roy was a ten-year assistant at North Carolina when Dean Smith convinced Kansas AD Bob Frederick to give him a shot. It happened at North Carolina when Dean retired and handpicked his assistant, Bill Guthridge, to be his successor. Obviously, both schools were able to see certain qualities in both candidates.

Think about it—if schools and athletic directors did their homework like Frederick did when he hired Williams away from North Carolina, they would be shocked to find the number of qualified, quality guys who are ready to step up. It's all about taking a chance.

Somebody from Georgetown recognized John Thompson when he was at St. Anthony's High. Somebody from Duke recognized Mike Krzyzewski when he was at West Point. Somebody from Seton Hall recognized Tommy Amaker when he was an assistant at Duke.

It's a bigger risk when schools decide to take a chance on a high school coach. Georgetown hired John Thompson right out of St. Anthony's High in Washington, D.C. In that case, we're talking about a very rare individual, a guy who commands respect in the community and at the university. And remember, he had some great credentials. He was an All-American at Providence and had played for the Boston Celtics.

The ideal way for a coach to move up these days is to serve as an assistant in a major program. If he can get on the staff at Kentucky, North Carolina, Kansas, Duke, Indiana, he's got a chance of something happening.

The other way to move up is to be a mid-major coach and get your team to the Big Dance. All of a sudden, you're a celebrity. And if you win a couple of games, you're even bigger. Look at Dan Monson who gained fame for his success at

Gonzaga in the 1999 Tournament which led to his landing the Minnesota job. Herb Sendek is another example of that after he took his Miami of Ohio team to 21 wins and a 1996 NIT bid. His reward? The head-coaching job at North Carolina State.

A successful coach has to pick his spots. Not every job is a good job. Mike Brey of Delaware has turned down a number of jobs. He's in a great situation and figures to make another run at the Tournament this year.

Some jobs are just waiting to be exploited. I thought San Diego State was a great job for a young coach, playing in a great location with great weather year-round. The Western Athletic Conference is a competitive league. There's no reason why the coach shouldn't be able to recruit one or two blue-chippers there every year.

I don't believe in the word "can't." When I was at Detroit, all I heard was concern over the crime. What recruit in his right mind would come to the murder capital of America? But you know what? That city had so much to offer. It had a great corporate base with the automobile industry, the school had no football team so basketball was king, and our program was on the front page of the *Detroit News* and the *Detroit Free Press* every day.

If a player wanted trees and grass, though, he didn't want us. But if he wanted to play basketball, get an education at a Jesuit school, get some name recognition in his state, Detroit was a viable option. If a kid played basketball there and went after a job at Chrysler or General Motors, they knew who he was. He had an instant resume because he had appeared so regularly in the local newspapers.

I think life was simpler then. Today, it's an unforgiving time, a bottom-line, what-have-you-done-for-me-lately world. Even at some of the traditional programs. Now that Tubby Smith has won a national championship in his first year in the Blue Grass, what can he do for an encore that will satisfy the old money in the stands at Rupp Arena? The banners at Pauley Pavilion will always haunt John Wooden's successors.

If you're in Indiana right now, no one cares about the national championships in 1976, 1981 and 1987. Everything is based on the here and now. And right now there are a lot of Indiana fans that seem to be very upset about what's happening down in Bloomington. That blows my mind. Add up Indiana's record in the '90's and you're still talking powerhouse. Has it won national titles? No. Has it been in the NCAA Tournament? Yes.

The Hoosiers had as long a run as anybody next to North Carolina. They've always been one of the most competitive teams in the Big Ten. But because they set a standard by winning national titles, fans identify with that, and that's all they want. Anything less won't do.

Indiana had a tough break in 1993 when star Alan Henderson got hurt. Otherwise, it had a great chance to make a run for the national title. It's not that Indiana hasn't had good basketball teams. The problem is that it hasn't had a great team. And again, fans get spoiled.

Star Luke Recker decides to transfer after the 1998-99 season and folks go nuts. Sure, the timing's bad on the heels of Jason Collier's transfer in the middle of the 1997-98 season to Georgia Tech, but folks, kids are leaving all over, and nobody's screaming about Mike Krzyzewski and Chris Burgess. Nobody's screaming about Adam Harrington down there with Herb Sendek.

Does Knight deserve some of the criticism? Obviously, and he'd be the first to tell you. One thing I love about him is that he demands the most out of his players. He demands that they go to class. He demands that they graduate. He demands they work hard. That's basically what he believes in and stands for.

He does have a way about him, and there's no doubt his style isn't for everyone. Because of that, his number of potential recruits is going to be smaller than the recruiting base of some other schools. Some kids are not going to buy into his philosophy and his way, and I think that hurts him in the recruiting wars.

The General is from the old school, and a lot of what's happening today really disturbs him. He's told me, "Dick, I can't believe I'm coaching in an era of long pants, earrings, the hair, the flashy posses. All this is everything I never believed in."

Bob Knight believes in fundamental, solid team basketball...pass, cut, screen, fight through the screen, help out on defense, communicate, and play hard. He always believes in the present versus the past. A player may start one game and not play well, and the next game he's on the bench. Is it right? That's for a player to evaluate and judge when he goes there.

I think any prospect that signs with Indiana knows what to expect. Am I saying Bob's right? No, not all the time. And it may not be the right program for some kids, so they should go elsewhere. There's nothing wrong with that.

In many cases — I won't say all because I exempt Duke and Kansas — I think it's opportune for a coach to check out after seven years. I think that after that, you wear out your welcome as a coach. Either you've spoiled the fans so much that they want instant success every year, and it's so tough to give it to them, or you become your own giant killer if you come into a program and you're successful right away.

I think sometimes a coach should go somewhere new, where he's treated like royalty. I think it's good for everybody involved, both the school and the coach. There are only a certain number of programs where a coach can year in and year out have a legitimate shot to compete and win. And even then, coaches tend to be judged by what they do in March. That's the one negative about the NCAA Tournament. It has become the criterion for defining whether you've had a successful year. That's sad.

Look at Kansas when Arizona beat them in 1997. Kansas had a phenomenal year. Every player graduated from the 1997 team — Jacque Vaughn and that crew. The Jayhawks won big-time. They were ranked No. 1 in the country all year. They get upset in the Tournament by Arizona, the team that ultimately wins the national championship. And all Roy Williams had to live with was "What happened in the Tournament?"

Same deal with Duke after it lost to UConn in the 1999 Tournament. Duke fans will not believe this, but I've had so many people approach me since the Blue Devils lost to Connecticut and say, "What happened to your Dukies? What happened to Duke, the team you bragged about so much during the year?"

What happened to Duke? They lost to a very good Connecticut team, and they were 37-2. For a lot of coaches, if you go 37-2 they build monuments for you. But they weren't building monuments for Roy Williams and Mike Krzyzewski after those two Tournament runs.

Whose fault is this? We're all guilty. I'm guilty, everybody in the sports world is guilty of getting so wrapped up in March Madness that the season is almost an afterthought. The Tournament has become like the NBA.

I don't care what your regular-season record is in the NBA. You can tell me about the great record the Utah Jazz posted under coach Jerry Sloan with the talent of Mr. Malone and Mr. Stockton. Do you think anyone cared about it when Portland bounced them out in the second round of the 1999 playoffs? The Trail Blazers sent the Jazz home. Boom. It was all over, just like that.

For Gonzaga, the College of Charleston, or Detroit (man, was it sweet to see my former school bump off UCLA in '99), just getting into the Tournament is big. And to win a game or two? Wow. For some schools, like Florida A&M, getting into the Tournament is like winning the national championship. For others —they'd better win six games. At Kentucky, do you think they want to hear about the Elite Eight? Do you think they say, "We had a great year, man, we got to the Elite Eight." Kentucky knows one thing: It's had so much success in a world of expectations, and that's what it lives by.

I did an interview with UConn coach Jim Calhoun after the '99 tourney and I said, "You know, Jim Calhoun, you didn't have to win the national title to prove you were a great coach to me."

When you look at what Connecticut has done over the last decade in the Big East — it's been as dominant as anyone. Look at how many times the Huskies came close — losing in the 1990 East Regional finals when Christian Laettner hit a dramatic shot at the buzzer, getting beat by eventual-champ UCLA in the 1995 West Regional finals, falling in 1994 to Florida in the East Regional semis when Donyell Marshall missed two free throws.

Calhoun was a brilliant coach in the eyes of his peers before he ever won a national championship, but this victory gives him validity. The visibility and the exposure he has received means his stock rises, as will his shoe deals and corporate endorsements. His reputation skyrockets.

As Jimmy Valvano always used to say, "There aren't many guys, Dicky V, who walk around with one of these." And then he would show me his championship ring. Think about it. How many coaches actually walk around with national championship rings? In the '80's and '90's, how many guys? Only sixteen, so once a coach gets that ring, man, it puts him in a very special club.

Coaches do a lot for the university, and yet they don't get tenure like professors do? Why? Years ago, Al McGuire suggested they should, and I agree. If professors receive it, why not coaches? I've heard the argument that it's because coaches make so much that the academic salary structure would have to be adjusted.

222

Hey, no insult intended here, but there is much more risk involved with coaching, the risk of getting fired. That's why coaches make more than professors. If there were tenure in coaching, it would make coaches schedule better.

People don't understand why coaches don't schedule all the giants. Well, a lot of coaches are insecure, worried about their future. They say, "We have to play enough tough clubs in our conference schedule, why should I go out and risk myself by playing this top-25 team or that one?" The coaches who have the mega deals and the guys who are on top don't care who they play. They can play anybody and it's not going to affect them.

Some people say coaching is a young man's game and that tenure would protect the older coach. I don't agree. You can't tell me John Chaney can't coach. I've watched him practice. The man may be in his 60's, but he can flat-out coach. I've heard it said that coaches get dumber as they get older, yet professors get awarded with all sorts of degrees and honors as they put in more years and get experience. What, as they get older they get wiser, but coaches get dumber? I don't think so. You tell me how a coach gets dumber. The game is what it is.

Jim Harrick said recently, and I agree with him, that John Wooden could coach today. "He would probably coach from the bench and not do all the traveling, but he has such a strong understanding of the flow of the game and the ability to make decisions on the bench, he'd be tough to beat." I don't think age alone is the determining factor, a lot of it comes down to the physical condition of the individual, how one takes care of his body, how healthy he is.

People ask me what makes an ideal coach. It's a combination of factors. He has to be able to communicate. He has to sell his program. He has to be able to recruit. He must be able to motivate. He must be able to handle game preparation and practice situations. If a guy can do all that and has some personality, he's close to the ideal.

223

Perhaps the greatest college coach ever, John Wooden is proof positive that age is not a deterent to head coaching success. Here he is with Louisville coach Denny Crum, who played and coached under Wooden at UCLA. Photo 9-5. (courtesy of University of Louisville).

A lot depends on whether a coach and a school are a good fit. Mike Krzyzewski and Duke are a perfect match because his philosophy fits with the school's academic mission, and he's been able to recruit the kids who mirror his beliefs. I'm not convinced Krzyzewski would have had the same success if he were coaching, say, a UNLV or a school that doesn't have the same atmosphere as Duke.

In college coaching, you must be able to deal with the media. Any guy who's a little glib, who can throw out one-liners and is popular with the media, can buy himself time in lean years. The late Jimmy V was good at that. Lou Carnesecca of St. John's was, too. If a coach like that has a bad year or two, the finger's not pointing at him because the local media likes him. But when a guy isn't humorous or can't excite the media with his personality, he'd better win.

Take a guy like Jimmy Boeheim at Syracuse. Here's a guy who lives and dies for his school, has produced exceptional teams. They should name the floor at the Carrier Dome after him for what he's given to the town and the university. If Boeheim posted 14-12 records — because he isn't exactly glib and funny — he would be in big, big trouble. But he wins 20 games and keeps the wolves from his door.

I also don't think that winning is everything. Coaches should be evaluated in one simple way; "Is he getting the most out of his players athletically and academically?" Every situation is not the same, so you can't look at W's as the only measure of success. Not every program operates under the same rules in terms of budgets, talent and academics. It's so unfair. I feel so guilty on the air at times — and I deserve to be ripped by other coaches at times — talking about the giants of coaching.

I'll say, "Wow, Mike Krzyzewski is a Rolls-Roycer. Roy Williams is a Rolls-Roycer. So are Tubby Smith and Nolan Richardson." But they have certain advantages that the little guys don't have. But life isn't perfect for them either. Education is going downhill, if we're to believe the latest graduation statistics released by the NCAA, which are discouraging at best.

Among all sports in the NCAA's annual survey, men's basketball has always been the worst. For the most recent group studied, those who matriculated in 1991-92 and were given six years to graduate, the numbers are horrific. Only 41 percent of men's basketball players graduated in the allotted time period at the 312 Division I schools.

That was the second-poorest showing since the NCAA began its graduation rate survey, starting with the freshman class of 1984. It marked the eighth-straight year that the rate for Division I male basketball players was far below the rate for all male students, which last year was 51 percent.

The numbers are somewhat misleading, however, because the NCAA counts players who transfer out against the original school, even if the player goes on to get a degree at another institution. What's more, the transfers who graduate don't count for the schools where they eventually get their degrees.

The NCAA refuses to count transfers because it would be impossible to keep up with similar numbers for the entire student body, although the athletes themselves could easily be tracked to academic conclusion. The NCAA says this is how the government counts it, and it uses the government's data.

Coaches freak when they try to defend graduation rates, what with transfers and the rash of underclassmen leaving early for the NBA. They aren't removed from the initial number and count as a "did not graduate." North Carolina has had more than its share of players leave, but many have returned to get their degrees. It can be done.

Let's hope that starts a trend. Bill Brill of *Basketball America* conducted a study on the nation's top 25 teams, as of their rankings in January 1999, and came up with these graduation figures, shown in the following table, based on freshmen who entered in the fall of 1988 though the fall of 1991;

At The Top		At The Bottom	
College	**Percent**	**College**	**Percent**
Stanford	100 %	Cincinnati	0 %
Indiana	87 %	Temple	9 %
Duke	83 %	Clemson	14 %
N. Carolina	77 %	Arizona	15 %
Xavier	77 %	Arkansas	18 %
Michigan St.	67 %	Maryland	23 %
UMass	57 %	Syracuse	25 %
Kansas	50 %	Oklahoma St.	27 %
Purdue	50 %	Connecticut	29 %

Coaches are coming under more and more scrutiny all the time. They are evaluated not only by wins and losses, but also by whether they run a clean program, how they act on the floor and by their graduation rates. That's only fair. But every scenario is different.

Cincinnati has always been at or near the bottom of the survey. The school itself had graduated 54 percent of its student-athletes but none of its male basketball players. But Huggins thinks the graduation rate may be skewed. He points out that the Bearcats recruited seven players during the year in question, 1992.

Terry Nelson and Erik Martin graduated but didn't count in these statistics because they were junior college transfers. Another, Shane Komives, stayed 25 days before transferring to Bowling Green, where he too graduated, but doesn't count. Two more, Nick Van Exel and Cory Blount, left

I truly admire coach Mike Montgomery who has a tremendous 100% graduation rate at Stanford, one of the premier academic powers in higher education. Yet his Cardinal team is always competitive in the Pac-10 and national scenes. He's doing something right! Photo 9-6. (courtesy of Stanford University).

school early for the pros and now are NBA stars. A sixth, John Jacobs, dropped out and works for a local car agency. The seventh guy, LaZelle Durden, wasn't eligible due to Proposition 48.

Huggins has been vigorous in defense of his graduation rates. Cincinnati has graduated 14 of 33 players since Huggins arrived ten years ago. Nine more are playing pro ball. Two others are enrolled at UC or elsewhere, finishing up their degrees.

A coach has a responsibility to speak to his players on the importance of education, and I think most coaches do. To me, the accountability of coaches for graduation rates has been so blown out of proportion. Accountability rests with the kids. Are professors held responsible for people who don't make it through their classes? Come on now.

A coach should certainly be accountable for the kind of student-athletes he brings into his program. He should make sure they have the support system they need to graduate: tutoring help, guidance counselors who make sure they're taking the right courses. Every program has to be judged differently on academics.

Coach K will be the first to tell you, "Hey, at Duke, we have a high graduation rate. Well, why shouldn't we when you look at what we're bringing in and what we're all about."

John Chaney has a different mission at Temple. I read that Kareem Abdul-Jabbar was talking about the benefits of Proposition 48 and ripped Chaney for his opposition to setting academic standards for freshmen. Abdul-Jabbar was critical that Chaney has graduated only 15 percent of his players since he starting coaching there. It really blew my mind because I don't think Kareem knows what John Chaney is all about. Chaney is into giving kids chances.

I'm guilty, and I think a lot of guys in the media are guilty when we talk about great coaches and great programs. We don't take into account that it isn't a level playing field.

Many times, Chaney is taking kids who might be more at risk academically. They have some skills, and maybe through his guidance and discipline they can make it. I've been at his practices. I know Kareem has never been there. He's never seen what those kids learn in a one-on-one session when Chaney's addressing them. I thought Kareem's comments were totally uncalled for.

Is there anything that can be done to improve graduation rates? Yeah. Recruit better kids, kids who are prepared for college and not just worried about jump shots falling. I blame the system and I blame the school.

But sometimes even that doesn't work. The way graduation rates are calculated is outrageous. I'll give you an example. Are you telling me Duke should be penalized because Elton Brand goes pro early, or Burgess transfers or Avery goes early? I can just see the headline: 'Duke graduates less than 20 percent.' Now, that looks great. Are you going to tell me that that's a true evaluation of the Duke system? No way. That just doesn't make sense. It's not logical, not valid.

A lot of times, college presidents talk the talk — about bringing in quality kids who will graduate. But sometimes it's the coach who has to walk the walk —to the unemployment line. Coaches are being fired at some really, really solid schools. They're being fired not because they walk in and say, "Hey, Mr. President, all my players graduated. Hey, Mr. President, none of my players got into trouble." They're being fired because the president says, "Hey, Coach, you were 4-18. It's time to say bye. The alumni aren't happy."

Administrators talk about the importance of graduation rates. But I guarantee you if a coach is 24-4 and a couple of kids don't graduate, they'll find an excuse to give him a five-year extension. That's just the way the system goes.

Coaching is much tougher today than it was in my era because everything a coach and his players do is in the public eye. The media put a lot of pressure on coaches. The radio talk shows just can't get enough information on recruiting.

230

The fans are hearing and talking about it all the time. Everybody thinks he's an assistant coach.

Fans don't want to hear about another school getting the edge over theirs. North Carolina fans don't want to hear about Duke's great recruiting class, that immediately puts heat on Bill Guthridge over at Carolina. And the media make a big deal any time a coach gets into a confrontation on the sidelines.

As if the graduation rates, recruiting, boosters, presidents, fans and media weren't enough for coaches to deal with, sometimes referees get involved in the fray.

Cincinnati started off the 1998-99 season with 16 straight wins before playing UNC-Charlotte. With 17.5 seconds left in the game, the 49ers had a two-point lead. UNCC guard Diego Guevara stepped to the line with a chance to lock up the game, but he missed the front end of a one-and-one. Cincinnati guard Melvin Levett rebounded the ball, raced down the court and drilled a three-pointer that would have given Cincy the lead.

But the officials ruled the shot didn't count because official Tom O'Neill inadvertently had blown his whistle, thinking Guevara was entitled to two shots. Three days later, Conference USA Commissioner Mike Slive met with Dale Kelley, the league's coordinator of officials, to review the play. Breaking the league's policy of not commenting on officials, Slive issued a statement indicating the ball was live after the missed free throw, and play should have been allowed to continue.

"We're always preaching to our kids to play 40 minutes," Huggins said. "Coaches are supposed to coach 40 minutes. The same should apply to officials."

Don't get me wrong. Officials have to be given the power to make calls without feeling like they'll be evaluated every time coaches disagree with them. These guys are trying to do an honest job. It's not easy blowing that whistle. The pace of

231

the game has gotten so quick. The size of the floor is the same, but the players are so much bigger and the bodies are so much more active. With the contact, the emotion and what's at stake, it's all out front.

By the same token, officials should be held accountable. If the media have questions after a game, I think the chief official should address them. Give him a five-minute period to respond. I think most officials would like to do that, but they're so tied up by their rules that they live in a shell, and that's not good. Let the officials be part of the forum. They're an important part of the game.

I like what they've been doing in the ACC since the 1998-1999 season. Fred Barakat, the head of the officials there, does an outstanding job of coordinating his officials. For big games, the ACC has been sharing the officiating with referees from other conferences to ensure that big-time officials are at big games. I think that's healthy.

People say they see the same officials doing six games in seven days, which is too many, there's no question about that. But at the present, there's no way of limiting the games officials work because they make their own schedules. The only way you'll change that is if you pay full-time salaries for officials. That means we'd have full-time officials. It would help tremendously if we did, but where do you get the bucks? You're talking some serious money.

Most of the officials have day jobs. People have to understand they're professionals. Most are principals, coaches and teachers. These guys are making some serious money at their "real" jobs. They're not going to throw these jobs and the security down the drain unless they were to get some good money for officiating. You're talking $75,000-$100,000 a year for these guys to make that kind of transition.

Would they be better if they could spend all day evaluating, looking at film on days when they're not working? Of course. Their schedules could be a little tighter too. I 'd like to see a national group for officials, with a commissioner at the head of it, whether it be Hank Nichols, who certainly knows a great deal about officiating, or someone equally qualified.

The commissioner would be aware of what's happening in college basketball across America. He would assign officials to certain games, even though, traditionally, that's been handled within conference play. There could be four assistant commissioners working in different areas of the country: the East, the West, the Midwest and the South. These assistant commissioners would report to the commissioner on what's happening in their areas. They could make sure refs are appointed to games based on the quality of their officiating and constantly evaluate them.

One of the toughest things for refs to deal with is coaches on the sideline. Without a doubt, coaches should be responsible for their sideline behavior. Coaches have to stay within the rules. Some are a little crazy. I tell you, I was the wackiest. A coach is going to do what he can to gain an edge with an official in terms of getting a call to go his way. I was fortunate that there was no cable TV in my era because I was a madman. I never wanted to let that guy on the other sideline think he had the edge on me.

You're always paranoid as a coach. You feel every call is going against you. That's not the way it is. In most cases, the passion that coaches show adds to the beauty of the game. The football coach is lost in the crowd of all the helmets and shoulder pads. In baseball the manager can't easily be seen, he's hidden in the dugout. But in basketball, he's right out there on the floor... naked, man. Everybody in the stands can see him. The fans can see his every movement and action, every jubilant moment, every sad moment, every feeling of excitement, every feeling of anxiety, every fear, the fans can feel that. And you don't like to see that part of the game taken away during a frenzied moment, so a referee has to use good judgment before he slaps a guy with a technical foul. Let the guy have his say, then just walk away.

Sometimes, coaches lose it when the fans get out of control. Bob Knight was offended by Northwestern fans chanting "Who's your daddy?" at him. Or was it "Hoosier daddy?" After Indiana defeated Northwestern, 69-62, he pointed to the scoreboard and repeated the same chant to the bleacher section nearest the bench.

"I just asked them, 'Who's your daddy now?' " Knight said.

Knight confronted Kevin O'Neill at mid-court and lectured him about the crowd. As Knight started to walk away, O'Neill grabbed Knight's trademark red warm-up before Knight ripped his arm away. Less than an hour later, the two cooled off and made peace.

But Knight had the last word, "That type of thing should not be part of college basketball."

And he's right. "Who's your daddy?" has become a common cheer among fans. Sometimes fatherhood is involved, sometimes it's a genetic putdown and sometimes it's just a play-on-words. Always creative, the Dukies serenade their own forward, Shane Battier, with, "Who's your daddy, Battier?" Sheer poetry.

Face it. Everybody tries to play for the camera, and everybody wants to get on TV, and everybody wants to make headlines. Kids are sitting up at night trying to create ideas. They see the Cameron Crazies, they see the Dukies going bananas, and everybody wants to top it. At different arenas I've visited, the fans will say to me before the game, "Wait until you see what we're like here, man, at our place. This is going to be really wacky."

I think University of Virginia and Duke fans and their pep bands have been leaders of the creative cheers. Other schools try to imitate them, some more successfully than others. I went to Stanford to do a game when they hosted UConn, and the Sixth Man Club got carried away, chanting "Deadbeat dad" at UConn guard Khalid El-Amin, who's a father of two. That was out of line. It's the school's responsibility to make sure that stuff doesn't happen and to reprimand the fans. The coach is doing his best in preparing his athletes to play. He can't be preparing every fan on how to behave.

Isn't it really sad that games today require so much security? But let's face it, there are some wackos in the stands who don't know how to act. The home team has to be accountable, and the home team coach has to get on the microphone and make it known, loud and clear, that his team is going to be penalized with a "T" if it continues. If none of that works, then it's time to clear the arena, man. Let everybody pay for the actions of a few, and you'll see how quickly it'll put an end to all that nonsense.

Sometimes coaches try to make a point while trying to quiet down the home fans. There is no love lost between Cincinnati and UNC-Charlotte. When the Bearcats played Charlotte on the road, their players were pelted with coins as they walked to the locker room.

During the return match, the Cincinnati fans reciprocated. Huggins got angry and drew a technical, then grabbed the mike and told the fans to control themselves. He urged fans to single out anyone who threw anything onto the court so they could be ejected. He also made a vague comment about other schools in the conference "who don't have any class." "We have class here," Huggins said. Cincinnati won, 82-69, but the conference reprimanded Huggins for his comments.

What has happened to sportsmanship? Basketball's had its share of ugly incidents, but I don't think I've ever heard of anything quite as uncalled for as an incident involving a Wichita State pitcher and a batter from Evansville in the Spring of 1999. Evansville junior Anthony Molina was taking practice swings about 15 feet from home plate when he was drilled in the face by a pitch from Wichita State's Ben

Christensen. The ball fractured three bones around his left eye and seriously put into jeopardy Molina's baseball career.

Christensen, a first-round draft pick of the Cubs, said he threw toward Molina to keep him from timing pitches while on deck but never intended to hit him. That gave me chills.

Later, Christensen admitted, "My assistant coach told me if [a player's] timing the pitches, knock him down right at the batter's box, let him know you're the boss." That's lethal. That's almost committing an assault. That's going too far.

This much is certain: Dignity and respect seem to be on the outs, and I don't like it. I want to see a return to the days when kids respected the game, their coaches, the system and their opponents. I want to see us return to relationships built on trust and understanding. Heck, hard work and effort need to be worth more than a kick in the butt.

And last but not least, we need to reinvent the word "sportsmanship." It needs to stand for the way we're going to play the game under today's rules and realities. Look in the mirror and ask yourself, "Is that the way I want others to treat me?" If you say yes, that's all you can do. That's where we need to go.

Is Michael the best of all time? Several members of the New York Knicks probably think so after he dumped 51 on them during a 1997 game at the Garden. But will I see another Jordan in my lifetime? I don't think so. Photo 10-1. facing page (AP Photo).

Chapter

10

Cinderella,

Where's the Ball?

College basketball must embrace the NBA's
concept of marketing to survive

In 1984, a basketball visionary named Sonny Vaccaro
convinced Nike, his employer at the time, to take its biggest

gamble ever and sign a player about whom even he knew very little. Vaccaro, working in Nike's college and grass roots division, had begun to make a name for himself after signing Georgetown coach John Thompson to his first shoe contract.

He had become intrigued with a somewhat scrawny guard at North Carolina, a dazzling freshman named Michael Jordan. He sensed something special about the kid and got all the proof he needed in the 1982 NCAA title game between Georgetown and North Carolina.

Along with millions of TV viewers, Vaccaro watched Jordan nail a jumper from the corner in the final 15 seconds to give the Heels a one-point victory and hand Dean Smith his first national championship. Vaccaro saw superstardom, and he urged Nike to go after him hard even though Jordan was only the third pick of the 1984 NBA draft.

A lot of the people at Nike originally were opposed to bringing him in, but Sonny made it happen. He sold Nike on Jordan's personality, potential, upside and way of dealing with people. Breaking with tradition, Nike eventually signed Jordan to a $1 million contract over five years and then gave him his own line of sneakers, called Air Jordans. At the time, Kareem Abdul-Jabbar was the only NBA player making six figures, a mere $100,000 at that, from a shoe deal.

But the investment was worth it. As we all witnessed, Michael Jordan became the greatest player in the world. He combined his unique style and flair, charisma and exciting play with personality. He had that unique combination, but he also backed it up with productivity; six NBA titles and two Olympic gold medals and countless individual accolades.

Jordan captivated the nation with his talent, success, demeanor, looks, style and presence. He is so polished. During TV interviews he always looks directly into the camera, always smiles, always has something of great interest to say. He could put his name on trashcan lids and the suckers would sell. There's no doubt in my mind he's the greatest ever to play the game.

By the time Jordan retired on January 13, 1999, he had made $130 million from Nike, but he brought billions into the business. Jordan sold $2.6 billion worth of basketball shoes with his name on them. He had become so successful and astute at business that Nike hired him as the working CEO of its Brand Jordan division.

Nike believes his name and charisma will continue to attract customers worldwide, and with good reason. Jordan has become a brand name overseas, even in places where basketball isn't king. Last year, sales of Air Jordans reached $350 million. That's almost 4 percent of Nike's $9.2 billion in revenue.

I remember watching a Michael Jordan interview with Larry King. You'd have thought King was talking to a CEO of a company. Michael talked about all the things he has learned while playing basketball and how the sport opened doors he never dreamed of.

As he said to Larry King, "Let's not kid anybody. If it wasn't for basketball, I would never have had the opportunities to learn what I have in the business world because it's given me a chance to sit with board of directors, to sit with brilliant business people, and share concepts and ideas."

He took advantage of that. I see too many athletes who don't capitalize on their opportunities. They just get isolated in that little world of shooting jump shots, hanging with the guys, and don't branch out. But Michael did.

I haven't seen anyone better than Michael at marketing a product. Tiger Woods has certainly taken the world by storm and brought the spotlight back onto golf with his dramatic entrance, but he has a long way to go before he'll have the impact of a Michael Jordan in the business world.

The only athlete I've ever seen who's had a similar global impact is Muhammad Ali. Ali's still a marketing machine. They're building a Muhammad Ali museum and a theme restaurant in Las Vegas. He's wanted for all kinds of commercials. His legend continues to grow and has been sustained over many years.

The question about Michael is will he continue his dominance in marketing now that he's not playing? Obviously there has to be a little drop-off, but I don't think it'll be that much because he's such a legend. His name will still have clout. He'll be more selective in what he does, but with his own line of clothing and merchandise, he's not going away any time soon.

At one point, Michael was very upset about the price of his sneakers and the labor practices in the facilities that make his shoes. It really bothered him and still does. He vows to visit Asia to tour the factories where his shoes are manufactured and make sure things are running properly. In an interview, he's said that if they weren't, he wouldn't think twice about leaving Nike. He is very morally sound in his business beliefs and business acumen.

Although a geography major at college, Michael has become a heck of a businessman. The *Wall Street Journal* has become a big part of his life. Michael will always be the man at Nike, but the search for his successor labors on, and in the forefront of that search are Nike and Adidas.

It'll be mighty tough to find the next Michael. But like anything else, ultimately, down the road, there will be another superstar. That said, I don't think I'll see it in my lifetime. In fact, I know I won't. I'll never see anyone who captured our imagination the way he did. You couldn't even compare him to the rest of the league. While others were All-NBA, he was All-Universe.

We can talk about all the great new kids; Tim Duncan, Kobe Bryant, Kevin Garnett, Shaquille O'Neal, but they've got to come a long way because, remember this, Michael put six championship rings on his fingers. That's tough to do in this era, to win consistently in a league that has star players jumping from team to team every year.

I've always loved watching Michael Jordan play. He owned the airways when he played for the Chicago Bulls, and helped make "sports marketing" a household term. Photo 10-2. (AP Photo).

Had he not won as much, would he still be as big a marketing machine? No, but he'd still be bigger than any other player because he's unique. People took notice because he did it with flair and class.

After Michael retired, I remember watching a farewell special on ESPN with my wife, Lorraine. I was totally in awe. I said, "Do you believe what we're watching?" as we saw high lights of some of his patented moves: double-clutches, hanging in the air, reverse jams, spinning, jamming from the foul line, monster dunks.

I sat there thinking, "There's no other human being who can do this." Then there was the clutch jumper, the last shot he would ever take, to beat Utah for his sixth and final ring. It was like Ted Williams in his last at-bat, a home run with the Red Sox.

Nike might go in another direction now that the U.S. Women's World Cup team has struck a chord with the American public. Nike's already locked up the star of that team, Mia Hamm. She is the world's all-time leading scorer in women's soccer.

She became famous from the *"Anything You Can Do, I Can Do Better"* Gatorade commercials she did with Michael. She also has a Nike TV commercial and MasterCard newspaper and magazine ads. She has a Mia Hamm Barbie doll and an autobiography titled, *Go for the Goal: A Champion's Guide to Winning in Soccer and in Life.* She even has a new 450,000-square-foot research and development building named after her at Nike headquarters.

From a women's sports standpoint, Hamm is very, very attractive to marketers. Soccer is beginning to grow, and that international acclaim will help her immensely. She possesses a lot of Michael's traits. Isn't it ironic that they both went to North Carolina? Is that the common denominator?

I got a chance to meet her once at a restaurant in North Carolina. I was in town to do a basketball game, and she was at the next table, and we wound up talking for a few minutes. I was so impressed with her and the way she carried and handled herself. She has the looks. I don't know much about soccer, but friends tell me she has all the moves on the field. She's soccer's answer to Michael Jordan. Nike has a great belief in Mia.

Nike is betting that Kevin Garnett or Tim Duncan, who was the MVP in the 1999 NBA Finals, will be the basketball heir apparent. But Nike isn't the only presence in the marketplace. Adidas pulled off a coup when it signed Pennsylvania high schooler Kobe Bryant to a $10 million contract right out of Lower Merion High in 1996.

The next year, it did the same thing with Tracy McGrady, who is making $12 million over six years. And the guy behind these deals was none other than Sonny Vaccaro, who left Nike in 1991 and went to work for its biggest rival. Adidas employs a grass roots approach, and Sonny is trying to recognize the potential of a young superstar and hope he'll grow. With athletes, you roll the dice. Sometimes it works, sometimes it doesn't.

But Adidas has a good one in Kobe. I think he has true potential. What his critics fail to realize is that this kid bypassed college but is still scoring around 20 points a game in the world's greatest basketball league.

I love listening to some of his comments. He patterns himself, whether he agrees or not, after Michael, in the way he dresses, the way he carries himself, the way he communicates, even the way he wags his tongue. And I agree that imitation is the sincerest form of flattery, there's nothing wrong with learning from the great ones that precede you. I see the similarities there, the potential for greatness.

Now what Kobe has to do is take his game to the next level. Kobe has to win. If he starts winning championships with the Lakers and if he starts putting rings on his fingers, you'll see his marketability explode. Of all the players in the game today, he's one who really handles the camera well.

He also comes from a great family that has had a very positive influence. His mom and dad are highly educated and well traveled. Kobe grew up in Italy, speaks two languages and has a great support system around him. His dad, Joe "Jellybean" Bryant, played pro basketball in the '70's and '80's and knew how to help raise his youngster. In fact, Kobe's parents moved out to the West Coast with him and, among other things, got him a personal trainer so he'd stay in shape in the off-season.

Kobe already has All-Star on his resume, man. He played in that game at the Garden when he was only 19. What he needs now is a championship ring. Even Phil Jackson says Kobe reminds him of a mini-Jordan, and now, with Jackson aboard as the Lakers' coach, look for Phil to put a little bit of the Jordan stamp on this kid. Every high school player thinks he's going to be the next Kevin Garnett or Kobe Bryant. But is that realistic?

In 1998, when Korleone Young, a 6-7 forward from Hargrave Military Academy in Virginia, didn't project and decided to enter the draft, his agent at the time made phone calls to both Nike and Adidas, hoping to negotiate a lucrative endorsement deal. He was turned down by both and wasn't even drafted until the second round by Detroit.

Every great high school player believes he'll be the next young superstar, signing those enormous contracts. For just about all of them, it's a pipe dream, but all these kids believe it because there are too many people on the streets filling up their heads with visions of grandeur. They're not living in a realistic world. And that's sad.

Garnett and Bryant have been the exceptions to the rule. They have proven they can play. Garnett signed a $126 million contract extension and he was only 22. Minnesota vice president of basketball operations and NBA Hall of Famer, Kevin McHale has done a solid job trying to surround Garnett with the proper people, offering him the proper advice.

The NBA is hoping that its current crop of young phenoms, like Kobe Bryant, will fill the shoes of Michael Jordan. Photo 10-3. (courtesy *Indianapolis Star*).

But the biggest dilemma young stars have is dealing with all the leeches that come in when they smell the cash. They see all the mega dollars that these kids are making and they want a piece of it. All of a sudden out of the woodwork, people who don't know anything about the business world become the athletes' best friend. Why? Simple, baby. They're hoping this kid can take them to fantasy land.

Being able to weed out the phonies from your legitimate friends and allies is important. But not every athlete is capable of making those tough decisions. Life can be very difficult for many of these young "phenoms" who may come from homes in which they received little direction. So sneaker companies have to be very selective in their spokesmen. And they start focusing on players at an early age.

The rush to put young athletes in specific shoes dates back to 1977 when Nike hired Vaccaro to set up a grass roots basketball program. The shoe industry was a mom-and-pop operation back then. In 1984, Nike started holding camps and paying coaches. Nike originally had the market all to itself. Bob Gibbons, of All Star Sports Publications used to work for the company as selection chairman for its high school All-America camp.

He'd pore over hundreds of names, tapes and statistics and choose the best prospects for a free, week-long, 130-player summer camp held at Princeton University. Players would attend academic classes in the morning then play in the afternoon and evening. Coaches from every major college would show up to evaluate prospects. Sonny had vision with the summer camps, the same type of vision he had years ago when he ran the Dapper Dan Roundball Classic in Pittsburgh, the first national high school all-star game, back in the '60's. He hasn't gotten enough credit.

He takes a lot of heat from a lot of people because of the battles that have raged between the shoe companies, the players and the agents. But Sonny has also helped kids who are not the so-called "mega superstars" get scholarships to college. He's donated thousands of dollars from his all-star games to charities like the Boys and Girls Club or a homeless shelter or the Cancer Society.

He was one step ahead with Michael Jordan and he's always been one step ahead with the grass roots movement. He's a thinking man in the world of basketball. Nike dominated the camp scene until 1991. Then Sonny left after a falling-out with the company and went to work for Adidas.

That ignited an arms race (or is it a foot race?) that hasn't stopped. Nike has locked up about 30-35 of the top 40 programs in college hoops, giants like North Carolina, Kentucky and Duke. Adidas has Notre Dame and some of the most widely recognized college football program; Tennessee, UCLA and Nebraska.

When Vaccaro started a summer camp that ran the same week as Nike's, it created an instant rivalry. Nike couldn't just choose kids anymore; it had to negotiate for them. Vacarro says he's worried he's created a monster.

"There is no moral ground anymore," he says.

Vaccaro has always said that if Nike quit, he'd get out of the summer camp business too. If he had his way, Vaccaro would open up the recruiting period to include the entire year so that Nike and Adidas wouldn't have to schedule their events in the same three-week period.

That could take a lot of pressure off kids. Besides, he says, three weeks is not enough time to evaluate players. Vaccaro thinks that if the NCAA had its way, it would shut down the summer camps completely.

As it stands now, Nike and Adidas compete for the best players. Nike sponsors around 100 high school teams and 45 traveling all-star teams. Adidas sponsors 150 high schools and gives sneakers to 150-200 more. It also sponsors 60-75 all-star teams and has a budget of around $1 million.

The situation has become worse since former Southern Cal coach George Raveling joined Nike. Vacarro and Raveling used to be friends. In fact, George served as Sonny's best man at his wedding. Now they are at war and it really disturbs me because I happen to like both guys. But I guess I have a better chance of growing a head of hair like Hugh Grant's than seeing Sonny and George friends again. Why? It's just too competitive.

High school blue-chippers are forced to choose which camp and which tournaments to go to. A lot of that depends upon which of the sneaker companies sponsors their traveling team in the summer. Sonny certainly has his guys, his coaches who supply him with his players. George does too. And that worries me a little. You start hearing stories about high school coaches being paid to wear shoes.

But you try to look at the positives. Both camps bring in speakers to talk to the kids about academics and personal responsibility. They try to educate them as much as they can about going to class, improving their test scores. But there are shenanigans you don't like. You hear about guys trying to wheel-and-deal, to hustle kids to the camp that's willing to pay them the most money.

Nike and Adidas attract the best players nationally. But I'll always be a little partial to the Five-Star camp because one of the real characters in basketball, Howard Garfinkel, is a friend of mine. Garf flat-out got me my first job in college coaching after he heard me speak at a banquet one night in the spring of 1971. He called to tell me that he thought I belonged in college coaching. I was touched, but I also was realistic enough to know that I was already receiving rejection letters from colleges across America.

But Garf contacted Dick Lloyd at Rutgers and got me an interview even though Lloyd told Garf he'd already narrowed down his candidates and there was no shot. Garf assured him that once he met me, he'd hire me. He was right. I got the job, and for that I'll always be indebted to Garf. And let me tell you, he'll never let me forget it! He may not get the same amount of superstars, but he always has a packed house because Five Star is such an outstanding teaching camp.

The Nike and Adidas camps are different. They're for blue-chip players who want to showcase their talents against one another, try to improve their stock in the eyes of the recruiters and the recruiting gurus.

People say it's not important to perform well at those camps; the kids are there to have fun. But it is important, particularly because of the early signing period. Coaches are trying to lock up players early. There's been many a kid who thought he could go to a great university but because he didn't play well at camp, found himself on the backburner of the recruiting list at a given school.

Kids can climb the ladder too. I remember the year Tracy McGrady came out of nowhere — who ever heard of Tracy McGrady? — to dominate the Adidas camp.

Nike and Adidas aren't hosting these camps because they like to see kids play. No, they want them to wear their shoes. It's a win-win situation. It's a win for the players because they're getting a chance to showcase their talents in front of coaches from all over America and they're getting a chance to play with and against kids they've heard about. It's also a winning situation for the shoe companies because of the visibility and exposure they receive.

Not everybody is a fan of the summer camp scene, however. Bob Knight has suggested that the sneaker companies that sponsor summer traveling teams are using those coaches to steer prospects to colleges that have ties to specific shoe companies. Then, if the player is good enough to make the pros, they've got the "in" with that player.

The way I look at it is that the shoe companies are doing what they're supposed to do, selling their product. It's the American way. As long as they're not breaking the rules, if they can market their product and get great exposure, fine.

That's why I have no problem with Nike and Adidas running camps for the best players in the country. Neither charges a dime, as long as a prospect can provide his own transportation.

I always look at the glass as half-full rather than half-empty. I think it's a positive when kids can find out how they measure up against the top talent in the country. I've seen some quality coaches working with the kids, trying to get them to play with other people.

I've been to the SAT classes the kids take in the morning. These kids are off the streets, playing hoops in a controlled environment. These things are all positive. But I get concerned when I hear stories about the shoe companies recruiting 12-year-old kids.

And nobody needs to read stories about shoe companies trying to influence blue-chip prospects to consider signing only with a college that wears their brand. And I think there's some truth to the stories about coaches who feel indebted to the sneaker companies for all the help they've received. You know, the old, "I give you equipment and clothing, now you give me something in return." It's almost an unwritten rule. If somebody has given you equipment and money, you're going to give them the edge when it comes to signing that great player to a sneaker deal.

Sneaker companies are not concerned just with high schools, they're on the college landscape as well. And coaches have traditionally benefited from their ties with them. The money is no longer obscene, but rival companies are still competing to lock up top-25 coaches with lucrative personal services contracts that can make a coach like a Rick Majerus or a Mike Krzyzewski up to $500,000 a year from Reebok or Nike.

Because of recent budget crunches, a lot of mid-major coaches are getting squeezed out of the bonanza. The shoe companies still give away equipment, but they don't give the kind of cash they used to. They try to zero in on just the elite of the elite.

Most elite coaches are funneling back some of their sneaker money into athletics, and that's good. I think the school has a right to be able to scrutinize and evaluate the shoe deal. But it's still the coach who is responsible for the contract being initiated at that university. It's due to his success, so he certainly deserves a good portion of the money.

Boy, how times have changed. I remember when I was with the University of Detroit and the rep from Converse used to come in. Man, if we could get a free pair of shoes we were happy. Are you kidding me? "Wow! I'm getting some Cons today." Sonny was the first to pay coaches to wear a specific sneaker. The coaching fraternity should be indebted. He's made a lot of coaches millionaires.

Lately, Nike and Adidas have tried to lock up entire athletic departments. Shoe companies now supply all sports at a school with equipment. Now, if a particular team wants to wear its own shoe, it has to be handled within the university family. Again, I think that if a company is going to provide equipment and revenue to your school, you as a coach sometimes have to play ball.

They all make quality shoes. More and more colleges are wearing sneaker company logos. The "in" thing for Nike, Adidas and Reebok is to buy a school and supply all of its athletic teams with product...even Penn State has given in.

Adidas actually sued the NCAA to make logos on uniforms bigger, challenging an NCAA bylaw that restricts member schools to limiting a manufacturer's logo to $2^{1/4}$ square inches. Adidas lost the case and asked for an injunction, which was denied. A U.S. District judge ruled that the company had failed to show the likelihood it faced irreparable harm by adhering to the status quo.

Ohio State, which has a $59 million athletic budget, has changed the way schools do business in athletics by taking marketing ideas from pro sports. The biggest source of school income remains ticket sales at $19 million.

But the school is reaching out to corporate America for much more. Nike pays the biggest chunk, $9.3 million over five years, for the rights to outfit the entire athletic program with its shoes and apparel. That comes out to $850,000 in cash and $1 million in apparel and equipment each year.

The university also has a soft drink contract, with Coke, worth $500,000 a year. Another $2 million comes from the Ohio Stadium scoreboard sponsors like Honda, which pays $186,500, and Big Bear food stores and Huntington Bank, which pay $177,000 each.

Then there's the new Jerome Schottenstein Center, where the Buckeyes play hoops. The family of the late businessman donated $12.5 million for the naming rights to the complex and Value City arena. Huntington Bank donated $5 million over five years to the concourse, an entertainment and concession area circling the arena. Kroger food stores donated $2.5 million to set up the Ohio State Hall of Fame, and Nationwide Insurance donated $1 million for help with the terrazzo artwork at the entrances.

And we haven't even talked about scoreboard signage, luxury boxes or the 40-year seat licenses that go for anywhere from $4,000 to $15,000. That's a far cry from the three R's.

The Tostitos Fiesta Bowl, the FedEx Orange Bowl, the CompUSA Florida Citrus Bowl. Every postseason football event has a sponsor. Is that healthy, or is it survival? The Final Four was held at Tropicana Field in St. Petersburg. I just visited Coors Field in Denver. Every stadium is getting a corporate identity. I have no problem with it. If that's the way you can bring in more income, so be it. The more revenue that comes in, the more it helps the program.

Hey, we're in America. America is a free-enterprise system. As long as you're doing something legal and you're doing it in the right way and you're not hurting anybody, there's nothing wrong with it. That's the capitalistic spirit that exists in our country.

People say sports have sold out to corporate America. I say "sold out" is overblown. Even the rulebook allows for a school to earn money. I'm from the school that says if you can raise dollars in a legitimate way and you can bring it into your program, there's nothing wrong with that. I don't know what you're selling out. If you're creative and innovative in the world of marketing today, those are the concepts that are available, and you'd better get with the program.

Some marquee programs want to do even more marketing. During the recent NBA lockout, college basketball had the court to itself. Were they able to take advantage of it? No. While TV ratings were up, not all the coaches were pleased. Some felt an opportunity was missed.

"It cries out for a governing body for college basketball, so when opportunities do make themselves available, you take better advantage of them," said Mike Krzyzewski. "The marketing of our product is really at a low level," he added.

Former Iowa coach Tom Davis agrees, "You go to an NBA game and they're giving stuff away. You go to a college game and you get nothing. Maybe in the halftime show."

Tom Davis never went to a Dicky V basketball game when I was coaching. We tried to give everything away because we had to lure people into the arena. There's nothing wrong with schools giving away hats or T-shirts or minibasketballs to sell tickets. If nothing else, it helps get the name of the program out there.

The NCAA is taking note. It's empowered a subcommittee to develop a marketing plan for college basketball. The NCAA's Dennis Cryder says committee and staff members considered a campaign to take advantage of the NBA lockout but decided to wait until the postseason.

After all, it's not like sports are becoming less popular in this country. With that in mind, conferences everywhere are looking to expand because of increased demands for more revenue, bigger network TV contracts. The Big East just added Virginia Tech. And the Big Ten and the ACC both discussed adding new members because they liked the idea of staging a lucrative conference championship game in football.

There was heavy speculation that the ACC might take Miami (Fla.), but the basketball coaches fought hard against that because they were concerned it might ruin the perfect round robin. Can you imagine a year when Duke didn't play North Carolina home and away? Besides, tickets to the ACC Tournament are hard enough to get. Add one, two, or three new members and you can imagine how all those big donors would feel if they got shut out because the allocation to each school decreased even more.

For a while, it looked like the Big Ten might take Notre Dame. The Irish were interested. At least, the academic side of the school was interested. But in the end, Notre Dame couldn't break with tradition...once an independent, always an independent. Amen to that.

If I had been involved in that decision, I'd have gone the same route. Notre Dame has such national recognition, why lock itself into one geographical region? In football, the popularity of the Irish is so great that the school can schedule teams all across the country. Financially, it has a bonanza with its groundbreaking TV contract.

As an independent, the school doesn't have to split any money with any conference, so it keeps all the revenue from bowl games. I think there would have been a lot of unhappy alumni if Notre Dame had joined the Big Ten. As it is, Notre Dame will stay independent in football and play in the Big East in every other sport.

There was some thought that the Big Ten might go after Texas or Missouri in the Big 12 or Syracuse and Rutgers in the Big East. Thankfully it hasn't happened. Big Ten presidents felt Notre Dame was the only school that had major leverage with the networks, and they didn't want to split revenue equally with another school unless they could be sure of that kind of revenue. Sometimes major conferences don't look at the big picture. They add teams regardless of geography. Whatever happened to natural rivalries?

And sometimes conferences lose perspective. When the WAC expanded to a few years ago, it was a nightmare, with the sixteen teams in two divisions spanning three different time zones. It was absolute chaos. Utah wasn't playing Fresno State every year. Now the conference has split up. There are eight teams now making up the Mountain West Conference and eight remaining in the WAC. Bigger isn't necessarily better. Sometimes a conference can get too big for its own good. It can lose its identity.

As the marketing aspects of college basketball are getting special attention, so, too, are such things as the length of the season. I think basketball starts too early. The Division One Working Group to Study Basketball Issues agrees and has recommended the season not start until after Thanksgiving and that there should be only 34 practice days before the games begin. Forget about those games in the second week of November. Football dominates the scene up to Thanksgiving.

Great basketball match-ups are taking place, but they're not getting the attention they deserve because everybody's caught up in the excitement of the great college football rivalries, the post-season bowl match-ups and the Heisman Trophy race. A few years ago, the presidents moved the start of games back to December 15 and practice to December 1. Then it was pointed out this would conflict with exams.

The NCAA has certain limitations involved in scheduling. The rule is that you can play 28 total games including regular season games plus a league tournament. The conference tourney counts as just one game, regardless of whether you play one or more games, so you can play 27 regular season games. Also, if you play in a tournament such as the Great Alaska Shootout, that also only counts as one game even if you play three. There are also exemptions, some are legit, some aren't. The preseason NIT, for instance, is exempted.

We run into situations where some schools have a terrific advantage because they take full advantage of the number of games allowed; 28 regular season plus tournaments, plus exempt games or a tournament outside the continental United States. I feel there should be a maximum of 30 games total, combining all the regular season, postseason tournaments and exempted games.

Last year, Duke's record was 37-2, that's 39 total games. That's a lot! How did they get to 39? First, they played 26 regular season games. They also played in two events that counted as only one game each, though they actually played three games in the Great Alaska Shootout and then three more in the ACC tournament. They also played one game in the Great Eight. And finally, they played six more games in the NCAA Tournament.

A program has to have a lot of success and a lot of visibility. The college game is getting bigger and bigger. The marketing aspect, while already successful beyond imagination with the success of the Final Four, is really just beginning to be tapped. Television coverage is incredible, perhaps to the point of over-saturation.

Years ago, you didn't have the choices you have now, what with the satellite packages and the growth of ESPN's sister channel, ESPN2. There are weekends when you can watch nine or ten basketball games. I remember when Brent Musburger and I were sitting in a room, before going to a really big game with Duke vs Carolina, thinking "Wow. This is great." When we looked at the TV pages in the paper, there were nine other games listed for that weekend.

Everybody is marketing like you can't believe. When I coached, schools didn't have marketing departments. Who had that in college athletics? I just hope it doesn't turn into the pros. It all gets back to money. Everybody wants a piece of the pie. And that's why when you go to an NBA game now, there's music blaring from the minute you walk in, there's all kinds of sound and lights going on throughout the game. Bulletin boards, scoreboards light up with advertising messages. It's entertainment mixed with athletics.

In the rush to make money, let's not forget that it's a game, and for the game to be successful you need to make sure the fans are happy. The players should be concerned about not losing that little kid who wants to be part of the scene, and stands out there but can't get in because the price of a ticket is so high. If you wanted to see one of the games during the 1999 NBA Finals between the Spurs and the Knicks, you had to be prepared to part with $300 of your hard-earned bucks.

The real fans —and the sport's future — are the kids on the street, but they can't afford to watch the games because all the season tickets belong to corporate America. Don't forget about the kids, folks! They're the fuel that powers the turbine.

And as the dollars keep driving the game, I simply caution the powers-that-be to be careful not to sell the game too far down the river. I think the NCAA's done an admirable job of marrying the financial realities with the association's educational mission by not allowing corporate sponsors to junk up the Final Four buildings with banners and flags.

They've tried to keep it pure in an increasingly muddy environment. Just keep it simple so that guys like me who just love the college game because it stands for competition, teamwork, loyalty and pride, can keep coming to the stadium and yell our lungs out for good old State U home team.

But in the end, I hope all the geniuses selling the game realize that no marketing gimmick can ever generate the goose bumps I got from watching the Connecticut players cut down the nets after winning that national championship in St. Pete. Young men, black, white, rich and poor, all scraping and hustling to play their best bring honor to the school, with a street-savvy winner like Jim Calhoun coaching on the side-lines, molding young players into men, giving them the confidence that they can succeed.

Watching scenes like that on campuses all over America is priceless. It's college basketball, the greatest sport on earth.

To put it in simple Vitalese... "It's Awesome Baby, with a capital '*A*!'"

Chapter

11

Millennium Milestones

*A game plan to restore pride and
integrity to college basketball*

Phew! Now, I know that's a lot to think about, but if we don't start taking positive action on these issues, the problems will only get worse.

My life has been blessed and I have had the good fortune to be part of the game at the high school level, the college level, the pro level...and now, in television. As I talk about the media, I have done so from the perspective of one inside the game. But, I realize that I am now part of the media; so I know I'm part of the problem, just as I may have been part of the problem when I let Les Cason stay on my high school team.

According to the *Providence Journal* in an article written by Kevin McNamara, Commissioner Michael Tranghese of the Big East lambasted the NCAA for the way it is overseeing men's college basketball. Tranghese who is highly regarded stated the sport is "out of control" and urged the NCAA to forget about all the bureaucracy and start to attack the many problems that exist.

Tranghese claimed coaches, administrators, athletic directors, etc. are totally frustrated. He went on to state that basketball problems such as player eligibility, player jumping to NBA, chaos with agents and recruiting irregularities are dominating the college environment. I say, Amen baby, to the commissioner's tirade.

Mike Tranghese was right on target when he addressed the media in New York about the many problems facing NCAA college basketball. I cannot agree more with Mike that basketball needs a special governing body with a leader to oversee every facet that is involved with college basketball. This group would report to the NCAA and truly represent college basketball in a positive fashion.

But I love this game and I want to make it better. I want to be part of the solution. With that in mind, let's summarize some of the issues we've examined:

- Regulate the transition from the college to the pro levels. The NBA Players Association has to work hand-in-hand with the NCAA to set a minimum age limit before underclassmen can turn pro.

- Legislate agent and booster controls that work for the good of the game. More states need to create laws that punish agents who compromise college athletes with illegal inducements. Universities need to monitor booster activities and send out a clear message that infractions will not be tolerated.

- Eliminate gambling, in any and all forms, from the game. Federal authorities need to step up their involvement in the battle against gambling on campus and prosecute at the grass roots level. Colleges should immediately wipe out eligibility for any athlete proved to be involved in gambling.

- Offer fair compensation to student-athletes and coaches alike. All coaches, especially those at big-time programs, deserve the money they make because of the pressures involved in the process of generating the high level of revenue they bring in to the school. But, it is equally important that the NCAA establish a tenable plan to pay a stipend to student-athletes in all revenue-producing sports.

- Uphold respectable standards for academic, moral and socially acceptable conduct. The Minnesota scandal, which involved a university academic advisor allegedly writing 400 papers for basketball players over a five-year period, should teach us a lesson about how things can run amok without a series of checks and balances. But players are responsible for their actions, too, on and off the court. There should be a no-tolerance rule in effect for violent crime.

- Set more realistic standards for academic performance from admission to graduation, primarily through freshman ineligibility. If schools are really interested in improving graduation rates, they should make freshmen ineligible. I've always been against using the SAT or ACT as a major determinant of whether an athlete can play as a freshman. By making freshmen ineligible, each school can control its admissions because players would have a year to prove themselves in the classroom. It might even help clean up recruiting.

- Take the necessary steps to ensure that all extra-curricular activities are a more positive influence on the game. Summer camps and traveling teams should be monitored but not necessarily eliminated.

- Establish a self-governing body to work in co-operation with the NCAA. College basketball needs its own governing body to control its sport. I'm not saying the NCAA should be shelved. It does, however, need to have a better understanding, and more consistent interpretation, of that 499-page manual. And most importantly, its rules need to start with common sense.

- Let's do more to open up competitive athletics to as many students as possible, especially to women. We should be encouraged by the fact that college athletics are indeed changing for the better; particularly women's sports, which have more scholarship opportunities than ever before because of Title IX.

- Something must be done about the great disparity in the vast numbers of highly qualified African-American coaching candidates and the shockingly few that actually have landed a head coaching job. In fact, I believe that universities need to be far more aggressive in considering all qualified minority group candidates for all staff and coaching positions in all college athletics.

- Everyone involved in the game must pledge to uphold higher ethical standards. As a matter of fact, I believe that the coaches and administrators have the same responsibilities as student-athletes to uphold moral and ethical standards.

- The self-governing body, along with the NCAA and member colleges, must create responsible marketing campaigns that will take the game to its highest level of potential. College basketball can't rest on its laurels, especially with so many stars leaving early. The game needs to be constantly marketed for the best results.

We need to take care of the student-athlete to ensure that the game remains pure. The game has to remain a game. There must be sportsmanship, respect, integrity and honest competition.

It didn't start out being all about money and TV appearances. It comes back to the essence of basketball, twelve guys on a team together with a coach striving for success. That nucleus comprises the beauty of the game. And as soon as you start diluting it, you get into trouble.

America is crying out for athletes who can carry themselves professionally on and off the playing field. I think that's why the farewells of John Elway, Wayne Gretzky and Michael Jordan really have been unbelievable. We've seen special documentaries on their backgrounds and careers.

To me, they all have a common denominator: They've withstood the test of time and they did it with an ultimate respect for the game. They've grown as human beings while playing the starring role. That's essential because if you consider that most athletes' careers are over by the time they reach their early 30's yet the average life span today is getting close to 80, these guys still have a lot of living to do.

Too many others aren't prepared for life away from the game. So many athletes let the game use them. Before they know it, the clock winds down and the game ends, leaving them hanging with little else but memories.

Too many guys have abused the system, and that's why we don't have as many sports heroes as we could — or that we have had in the past. We've been let down so many times.

That's why I think we need to make these changes at the collegiate level. It's while these kids are in college that they can learn life's crucial lessons that will help shape them and prepare them not only for a pro career if it beckons, but life in the real world after they tuck away their uniform for the last time.

And in the end, make no mistake about it; our focus should always be on the student-athlete.

The new millennium is upon us. And for the good of the game I love dearly, college basketball, we need to ensure that the future will be even brighter.

Let that be our legacy.